Women's Seclusion and

Men's Honor

CHAPTER 1

Introduction

PURDAH OBSERVED

Jawaharlal Nehru once told how surprised he had been by the response of Indian women in 1930 to Gandhi's call for the Civil Disobedience Movement. "I think that the most important and significant feature of that movement was the tremendous part that the women of India took in it. It was astounding" (Norman 1965: 412–13).

He succinctly stated his views on the status of Indian women in a speech he gave in 1949. "I am quite convinced that in India today progress can be and should be measured by the progress of the women of India" (ibid., II, 508). In ascribing such importance to women's status and conduct, Nehru was in agreement with traditionalist Indian Muslims and Hindus. Though they might disagree with every other aspect of Nehru's ideas about women, most of them would concur that the status of women is of great concern to each man and to all of society.

Nehru's astonishment at the staunch uprising of many women at Gandhi's call is more akin to the surprise expressed by Western observers when they find that demure and self-effacing Indian women may, in certain life situations and at certain historical junctures, take decisive action with spirit and determination. Indian men are usually not quite so surprised on such occasions.

Nehru was speaking of all of India. Our inquiry here is primarily concerned with the people of the north of the subcontinent among whom the separation between women and men tends to be more marked than it is among those in other parts of South Asia.

Women veil and seclude themselves before men through the large part of South Asia that includes Pakistan, northern India through Uttar Pradesh, and Bangladesh. They do so before certain kinds of men and not before others, in given social situations and not in others, and as one expression of a more general mode of conduct in which a woman's behavior directly affects the personal and family honor of the men closest to her. These men believe their honor and the linked demeanor of the women to be of central importance in their lives.

The most common term for these practices is purdah ("curtain," *pardā* in Hindi and Urdu). The term has been used narrowly, for specific traits of physical covering and spatial enclosure, but we here take the broader usage, which also includes the beliefs and values about the behavior of women, the restrictions on their movements outside the household and the requirements for their respectful and deferential demeanor within the home. Purdah is maintained by most peoples in regions of the northern tier of the subcontinent, the basins of the Indus and Ganges rivers. Among them, purdah is a constant element of everyday life; it symbolizes some fundamental values; it influences other parts of their cultures; it has important consequences for personality, economy, and society. A sketch of so important a feature in the lives of so large a part of the world's population must necessarily be done in broad strokes, emphasizing the general similarities rather than the myriad differences in detail.

These regions are here called the purdah regions. While there is much social and cultural difference between, say, Hindu or Sikh Punjabis and Muslim Bangladeshis, and the staple crop is wheat for the former and rice for the latter, it is useful to refer to both as being among the peoples of the purdah regions. The term purdah zone is similarly used here to include those regions of the northern parts of the subcontinent (except for Bihar and West Bengal) where purdah practices are taken to be central elements of social life.

There is no abrupt shift from a purdah to a non-purdah region, but rather a gradual transition through the intervening regions to the quite different gender relations of South India.

A family can properly practice purdah, as propriety is defined in its locality, only if its members can afford to do so. Those who must worry about their daily food (a large part of the population of the purdah zone) cannot support the full seclusion of women. But those of the poor who prosper commonly adopt more stringent seclusion.

In addition to this basic difference by economic class, purdah is carried on in two principal versions, one Hindu (and Sikh), the other Muslim. We first examine the elements common to both, then consider the differences between them. The common features, including factors of personality and socialization, are then reviewed in the broadest perspectives of time and space, in terms of cultural evolution and world area comparisons. The area of particular relevance, the Middle East (including North Africa), is given separate review.

Traditional purdah concepts and customs are still maintained among most peoples of the northern subcontinent. But these ideas and practices are everywhere being challenged by people's experiencing of modern influences. We will make some assessment of the contested and evolving responses, especially in urban and educated families, where the changes are most pronounced.

Veiling by women is so frequent, commonplace, and reflexive an action that it is scarcely noticed among these peoples unless it is not promptly and properly forthcoming. But when an English anthropologist, Ursula M. Sharma, came to study the people of a village in Himachal Pradesh, the practice struck her as "most alien and curious." She writes, "I found it disturbing when an informal conversation with a group of women was interrupted and my companions would veil themselves and become silent and restrained as an older man passed by the courtyard where we were sitting" (1978:218).

These were Hindu women; Muslim women also veil before senior men of the family. A woman quickly covers her head at the approach of an older man of her husband's family, using either the end of her sari or the separate head scarf, *dupatta* in Hindi, to do so. She draws the edge of the cloth across her face so that only her eyes are uncovered, or pulls the headcloth forward in a cowl from which she can peer out.

The gesture is but one feature of the mandatory code for a woman's conduct which requires that she behave modestly, restrained in speech, restricted in movement. She must observe, as Sylvia Vatuk puts it, "shyness of demeanor, avoidance of eye-contact with males, avoidance of loud speech and laughter (particularly in the presence of or within earshot of males), and the limitation of conversation with non-family males to necessary work-connected topics." A woman rises or shows other signs of respect within her home before male visitors as well as to older men of the family. If she is unavoidably in the presence of a conversation among men, she should not actively participate, and if she does speak she should cover her mouth with hand or cloth (Vatuk 1982:70). Far more than for a man, a woman's conduct, especially in traditional and rural settings, is expected to be constrained and, with relatively few exceptions, to be so in practice both inside the home and out.

Within the household, men and women often live, for the greater part, in separate places. They sleep in separate rooms or on separate sides of a hut; they relieve themselves in separate fields or locations; they sit apart at all social or religious occasions. Men spend most of their time in their own quarters, which may be a separate structure or platform, an outer room, a veranda, or, among the poor, just a cot set outside the house. There the men talk, smoke, work, lounge, entertain, and sleep; there a woman rarely sets foot. The women of the household remain apart in a courtyard or inner room where they carry on domestic and child-rearing tasks and in general spend most of their lives. Into these precincts a man of the family comes to take his meals, to do necessary chores, to exchange communications, and to share a bed briefly and quietly in the still of the night (cf. Minturn and Hitchcock 1966:21–24; Roy 1979:20–30; Pettigrew 1975:48–50).

Over time, a woman modifies some of her behavior showing respect. When she comes into her husband's parental family as a bride, she must be most diffident, shy, and self-effacing, quite unlike her far freer demeanor as daughter in her own parents' house. She keeps her gaze lowered, her voice still, her features covered, and her whole presence unobtrusive. She may even veil herself before her mother-in-law and perhaps her husband's brothers' wives. After a period of days or months, she begins to emerge from the bridal shell. After she has borne a child, she is likely to reduce some of her veiling, such as veiling before her mother-in-law (Jacobson 1970:137–40).

A young wife must appear completely uninterested toward her husband when they are in the presence of others. She must veil before him, and must not speak to him directly or even look steadily at him. A young couple must remain aloof from one another in public, and avoid direct communication until they can manage to be alone (cf. Minturn and Hitchcock 1966:34–35; Aziz 1979:56; Nath 1981:23). Only when couples become more senior in the family do they relax restraint between themselves in public (Jacobson 1970:140–43).

One relationship is relatively easy from the start—that between a wife and her husband's younger brothers. There is usually a casual joking relationship between them, and even newlywed wives can appear barefaced before these younger brothers (cf. Mandelbaum 1970:88; Aziz 1979:117; Nath 1981:24).

In sharp contrast, a woman should never stop sending signals of deference and respect before her father-in-law and her husband's elder brothers. Neither the passage of time nor the patina of familiarity should be allowed to blur these symbolic statements. A woman makes these gestures not only before the senior males of her married home, but also typically before the senior males of that whole village. Kinship terms are commonly used among fellow villagers of all groups. Even a man of lower caste-rank than hers may be called, through fictive extension, by the term for a husband's older brother. And a woman will veil before him as she does before the actual kinsman. Since there are many such elders, a daughter-in-law usually veils whenever she goes out of her house (cf. Freed 1963; Sharma 1980:6, 186; Aziz 1979:76–82).

Senior men, in turn, bear responsibility to keep their distance. If they have to enter the women's place, they usually announce themselves with a warning cough or some other signal. Messages to women are commonly carried in by children so that the court-yard need not be immobilized by the entrance of an elder male (cf. Minturn and Hitchcock 1966:34). About Muslim men in Delhi, Cora Vreede-de Stuers noted, "Curiously enough, I had more the impression that the men were excluded than that the women were secluded" (1968:42). Women do not encourage the men of the family to linger in their space. It inconveniences them and discomforts any women who may come to visit.

Outside her household, a woman's movements are restricted in distance, duration, and purpose. She should not venture out alone beyond the immediate vicinity of her home. She should not go beyond the village or town limits except for purposes approved by family elders and then preferably accompanied by a male kinsman. Women who must go out to work in the fields cannot be as closely circumscribed as those who do not. Work groups can include both men and women, but a woman laborer will be reprimanded if she strays out of the circuit of work and home neighborhood. In the fields she is likely to pull a cloth across her face in the event she might see an elder male approaching. Some household tasks, such as shopping, are often done by the men (or by servants in wealthier families), but may also be done by the women of a household. Such tasks should be carried out expeditiously, with as little tarrying as possible (Jacobson 1982:90, 94).

Sometimes a young wife is not allowed by her mother-in-law or husband to visit other homes. In his autobiography, Gandhi tells how as a young husband he insisted that his wife should not go out anywhere without his permission (1957:13). Doranne Jacobson gives an extreme example of a Muslim woman in a Madhya Pradesh village whose sister lived close by in a neighboring house, but the two women were never allowed to visit one another, because their husbands insisted that they remain strictly secluded within their own homes (1970:176). Some women take pride in their close confines. Ursula Sharma mentions a Hindu woman of a village in Himachal Pradesh who told her that she hardly ever stirred beyond her four walls. "Later I realized that it had been said in a spirit of pride. She did not need to stir beyond her four walls" (1980:43).

In religion, women have small part to play in events that are societal, transcendental, or public. They do perform major roles in domestic rites and conduct those ceremonies that are only for women. In some regions, certain women, usually from the lower-ranking groups, can become possessed and may act as shamans, but there is no claim that these performances have much to do with supernal forces of the high religion (cf. Mandelbaum 1966: 1176–77).

Women not only should avoid places where men congregate, they should also shun spaces where few or no people are. When a group of women cross wastelands or woods, they tend to quicken their pace lest they attract the attention of male strangers in places where, in case of attack, their cries might go unheard (cf. Sharma 1980:41–43).

Women's participation in secular public affairs is minimal. Many women now vote; exceedingly few, except for highly educated women, ever speak at public occasions. There are exceptions, and even in villages, voices in a higher register are beginning to be heard at local meetings, especially from women who hold official seats. Women's absence from or silence at such meetings is still the rule, however.

There are marked differences, as we shall discuss later, between a young woman's tightly controlled conduct as a daughter-in-law in the village into which she has married, and her easier, unveiled behavior in the village where she was raised and where she is always considered one of the daughters of the village. A Hindu bride in these regions must be married out of her childhood village. This is not necessarily so among Muslims; a Muslim bride who is married within the village does not undergo quite so dramatic a shift in her conduct.

In settings where a woman's conjugal family is not known and so its reputation is not so directly at stake, a woman can afford to be somewhat freer in her conduct. "When one is not in one's own place (*apni jageh*) one's neighbors do not have the same power to sanction." In towns, Ursula Sharma adds, there is enough anonymity about public places to make women more willing to venture into them if they have some business or purpose there (1980: 45). But in all outside places a woman must take care to keep herself guardedly aloof from contacts with men.

Sanctions on wayward behavior, real or alleged, can be severe. Neighbors' gossip about an unmarried girl may undermine her chances for a worthy marriage. A husband who suspects that his wife's conduct has damaged his and his family's honor may beat her. He may also refuse to allow her to visit her parents' home, a considerable penalty on a young wife. Perhaps worse, he may send her there and refuse to take her back. There she will languish, neither maid nor wife, until her natal kin can negotiate a resolution.

Muslim husbands can divorce a wife in the simple way prescribed by Muslim law, although the incidence is not as common as the ease of securing it might suggest. A disgruntled Hindu husband generally accomplishes the same purpose without any legal ado. A woman's daily guidance and reproofs come from the senior women of her family, particularly from her mother-in-law. When, in her turn, she becomes a mother-in-law, it is her obligation to see to it that her daughter-in-law maintains the rules and niceties of the kind of purdah that is proper to the family's status, wealth, and aspirations.

REASONS: SPOKEN AND UNSPOKEN

Why then must a woman send forth, within her own household, an unremitting stream of signals, day-long, life-long, affirming her subordination, restating her modesty? Why must she curtail her movements beyond her threshold, take care not to be alone abroad, avoid direct eye contact with men or any implication of inviting cordial personal relations? The answers come readily from the women and men even though this behavior is, for the vast majority of women, part of the given circumstances of their lives. Given, but not unchallenged. They are aware of challenges from various sources, from youngsters who must be properly socialized, from the example of the occasional village woman who, because of personality or circumstance, flouts some of the purdah rules, and from the implicit defy posed by those women, usually well-educated and Western-influenced, who walk freely about the streets with no more shield than a confident air and a pair of sunglasses.

Two kinds of answers are forthcoming, one about the dangers *to* a woman outside her home, another about the dangers *from* women inside their households. The contrast between outside and inside is a basic one. The title of a novel by Tagore (made into a film directed by Satyajit Ray), Ghare Baire, "in the house and outside" (*The Home and the World* is the English title), is a common and key Bengali phrase. Within her home, as Mary Beech notes for Bengal, a woman enjoys shelter, while "outside there is a lack of protection, a sense of potential danger, an insecurity. One takes risks in going outside" (1982:111–12).

Women are not expected to be able to cope with the exigencies of the outside world. The prime danger is from male strangers who are seen as liable to take advantage of an unescorted woman. Such strangers, as a category, are presumed to be sexually predatory and always ready to pounce. Some young men (and some not so young) reinforce that notion in town streets and in buses through the common practice known in Indian English as "eve-teasing." In the anonymity of the streets, some men who would spring fiercely to the defense of the women of their own families, leer, hoot, pinch, and make sexually pointed remarks at passing women whom they do not know and who do not know them (cf. Jeffery 1979:154–55). However, they rarely act that way in their own *mohalla*, neighborhood.

Assaults on women and rapes do indeed occur, perhaps as often in some places as in some Western societies. But in these lands, the dangers to women have heightened consequences. Women are viewed by men and view themselves as physically weak, perhaps sensually willing, certainly exceedingly vulnerable. A woman alone is unable, so it is thought, to withstand a stranger's sexual demand not only because he is generally bigger and stronger but also because her stringent training to be submissive makes her submit in these straits. Moreover, both women and men, especially when young, are considered to have uncertain control of their sex drives; people tend to suspect that assaulted women may, wittingly or unwittingly, have led a man on (cf. Vatuk 1982:59; Jacobson 1970:206).

If a woman does have an illicit sex encounter, whether by force or consent, and it becomes known, the shame may well blight the rest of her life. Village gossip frequently buzzes with rumors of illicit liaisons.* But when clear evidence becomes public knowledge, hard sanctions often ensue. In extreme cases, an unmarried, pregnant girl may be killed by her own father or brothers (cf. R. Freed 1971). An errant wife may be driven out of her husband's family, forever separated from her children. Others also incur grievous hurt by her default, be it voluntary or involuntary. The shame falls not only on the hapless woman. Her husband and all

---

* While local gossip often relates tales of extramarital sexual activity, it is not easy (at least for me) to gauge what may actually go on. In her study of a village in Madhya Pradesh, Doranne Jacobson found that despite the strength of purdah restrictions and the high importance of the ideal of female chastity, "many women engage in illicit relations in their conjugal homes as well as in their natal villages, where they observe no purdah" (1982:99–100; *see also* Jacobson 1970:128–29, 158, 202, 205, 368; Minturn and Hitchcock 1966:97–98).

A woman veils before a senior male.

in his family suffer grave dishonor. To fend off such consequences, women are kept and keep themselves guarded in movement and manner when they venture outdoors.

As for the display of deference and avoidance inside the household, the reasons given are phrased as the need to show respect within the family, and as the need to preserve the solidarity of the family. Both explanations imply a certain danger from the women; both have to do with domestic power and politics perhaps more than with concerns about extramarital sex within the joint family.

The myriad face-veilings and head-coverings before affinal kinsmen are made and received as signs of respect. They are acknowledgments of the right of the receiver to superior status and to priority of consideration. They connote acceptance by the sender of her subordinate role (Jacobson 1982:98). In the instant of response a woman does not ponder the meanings of her reflexive reaction when, say, her father-in-law comes into the room. But loud and lengthy excoriations about any lack of proper response will be directed by a mother-in-law to a negligent young daughter-in-law. Signals of respect are common in most face-to-face encounters. Thus a grown man may snuff out his cigarette in the presence of his father lest such self-indulgence be taken as lack of proper consideration of the father's status. A younger brother usually defers to his older brother in public even though the show may be quite cosmetic. It is as though people need to elicit the endless streams of respect signals because they see their societies as being innately and rightly hierarchical but with every particular hierarchy in need of active reaffirmation.

Muslim scripture decrees equality within the brotherhood of Islam. While Muslim women have important scriptural rights and equal opportunity for salvation, there is no more idea in Islam of complete social equality between the sexes than there has been in other world religions. Muslims, in these regions, like others of the Indian cultural sphere, share the assumption that hierarchy pervades gender as well as most social relations. So among all religious groupings, in all sectors and levels, most social encounters are presumed to be between a superior and a subordinate.

Yet the balance of hierarchy is felt to be precarious, especially between those who are close in rank. It is so within a family as among the groups of a locality, because people believe that those who are inferior in a given exchange will press to alter their lower positions if and when they can (Mandelbaum 1970:623–35). Hence expressions of general respect and specific deference are required at every sensitive point and moment.

So respect displays are flashed in many social contexts. They take on particular importance within a joint family because family elders tend to view an incoming bride as a potential threat to family solidarity. A bride comes to live with her husband in his parental household together with his brothers, their wives and children, and the unmarried daughters. Almost all village and many town couples live with the husband's parents, at least for a time. In some groups it is for only a few months, in other classes and castes for the lifetime of the husband's father and sometimes beyond. In the everyday interactions of family life, a woman defers to the men in many formal ways. At meals, a woman eats only after the men have been served. When a wife walks with her husband she follows a few steps behind him. Nazmul Karim writes of his Bengali Muslim community in his parent's generation that "in order to inculcate the habit of obedience a female newcomer (a new bride) was taught to salute her husband by touching his feet every morning before he went to work" (1963:304). Karim implies that this is no longer done in his community. It is not obsolete in other communities across these regions. Those wives who still make this ritual gesture would scarcely agree that it is enforced upon them but rather that they do it as an affirmation of respect, devotion, family harmony. In dedicating her major book (1965) to her husband, Mrs. Irawati Karve, the pioneering anthropologist, concluded with ". . . let me express my feelings in the traditional Hindu manner: I place my head on your feet and ask for your blessing." *

Punctilious deference by junior wives is considered to be essen-

---

* To those who knew this admirable couple—she a distinguished scholar, he a renowned educator—this dedication carried additional meanings. He was firmly supportive of her independent career; she was a strong person; their relations seemed to their friends to be like those of an academic couple elsewhere, with each partner able to work successfully in a different field. Mrs. Karve cherished much of the Hindu tradition.

Mrs. Karve once called my attention to a reference I had made to her in print in which I had not prefixed "Mrs." to her name. She let me know that she much preferred that the marital title be used. She wanted it understood that though she was a professional anthropologist, she was also a complete woman. Years later, an Indian woman of a younger generation, married to an American, rebuked me in a letter because I had put "Mrs." before her name in writing about her studies on fertility. When next we met she explained that though she was a married woman, in that context she should be identified only as a professional. Yet Mrs. Karve's ideas about the status of Indian women were quite like those of the younger generation of women scientists and scholars in India (cf. Karve 1966).

tial in a joint family where several couples must live close together with enough accord to function as a family. Hindu brides of these regions come in as strangers from another village. Each has her own interests and loyalties, as to her own natal kin, that are not those of her conjugal family (Jacobson 1982:97–98). Muslim brides are not necessarily strangers, but both Muslim and Hindu family elders tend to be skittish about signs of rift among the sons. They are likely to attribute family discord and difficulties to disruptive pressures from the wives.

To avert such separatist tendencies, a wife is required to keep at some social distance from her husband and children in the presence of others. Among Rajputs of a village in western Uttar Pradesh, "covering the face in the presence of one's husband is also a sign of respect for his mother, another of the customs designed to protect the mother-son relationship from being threatened by a son's attachment to his wife" (Minturn and Hitchcock 1966: 34). In the Madhya Pradesh village studied by Doranne Jacobson, a man should avoid fondling or carrying his own child in the presence of his elders. A woman also feels embarrassed to give obvious affection to her own children in full family view, although both men and women feel no shyness about playing with the children of others in the family. "Thus the special kind of interest and affection which might otherwise grow between a man, his wife, and children are subordinated in order to permit close ties to develop between members of different nuclear units within the larger family" (Jacobson 1982:98).

Respect-avoidance is also supposed to avert improper sexual attraction. "Presumably brothers are less likely to lust after each other's wives if the latter's charms are concealed from them" (Sharma 1978:219). This explanation does not tell why a woman may appear unveiled before her husband's younger brothers. One reason may lie in the greater power and authority attributed to an elder brother. Should an elder brother make sexual advances to a younger brother's wife, it might put the younger brother in so intractable a bind between his differing obligations as husband and as junior brother that he would separate from the joint family. But if an elder brother objects to an overly warm relationship between his wife and his younger brother, he can, presumably, scotch it promptly. In some caste groups of North India, sexual liaisons between a woman and her husband's younger brother are considered to be good for the family and to provide no cause for objection by the husband. If the husband should die, the explanation runs, the younger brother will already have emotional links to the widow and so will readily take responsibility for her and her children (cf. Pettigrew 1975:53).

The ideal of a large, harmonious, cooperative joint family is much cherished, but such families are known to be difficult to maintain and destined eventually to disintegrate. People prize the ideal for solid practical reasons. The most prosperous, socially successful, secure, admired families are apt to be joint. Nazmul Karim recalls that his father often held up to his children the example of a large Hindu joint family in a neighboring locality in Bengal. As many as forty took their meals together, it had more than a dozen university graduates, and its children excelled in curricular and extra-curricular activities. "My father used to say that the progress of that family had been assured by cooperation and joint action. . . . If the members of his family worked on the same principle, his family also would be as renowned as the Dattapata family" (1963: 306).

These were "progressive" townspeople, landowners and civil servants, Muslims and Hindus. The same esteem for the joint family still prevails among many villagers and some urban families. For them, jointness is the precursor of prosperity and power (cf. Nicholas 1965–66:39; Jacobson 1982:103). Close cooperation among grown brothers living in one household is, to begin with, economically rewarding. Cultivators in a joint family can divide tasks more efficiently, mobilize hands when needed, manage household costs more cheaply, negotiate better with local authorities, take over for a sick or disabled member and work the unfragmented family lands as a team. With the gains of their joint efforts, they are better able to acquire improved implements and, possibly, more land, to boost their wealth and status.

Moreover, village society is commonly highly competitive, violence not far offstage. A man's strength is enhanced if he is one of a band of brothers in a joint family. That concerted strength can be projected politically, or physically if need be, in the common struggles among village factions. With augmented wealth and power, a family can raise its social rank, particularly through arranging prestigious marriages for its daughters (cf. Mandelbaum 1970:104– 9; Pettigrew 1975:54–56). Another attraction of belonging to a large harmonious family was expressed to Husain by village-bred factory workers in Dacca: "There is more fun in living jointly" (1956:77).

But people also know well how difficult it is to attain and to maintain the advantages that come from living in a strong joint family. When brothers threaten to part, they are typically beseeched by their best-loved kin, by caste and village elders, to remain as one household. Yet centrifugal forces eventually prevail; the family separates; the possessions are divided. This occurs either during the waning of the father's command or not many years after his death (cf. Vatuk 1982:60; Jacobson 1970:80–81, 84; Pettigrew 1975:51, 53; Rizvi 1976:39–41). Blame for the separation is usually put on the wives of the brothers. Commonly enough, relations among the brothers have also become quite brittle, but the male bond seems to be too precious and too tenuous to be so impugned (cf. Lindholm 1982:120).

The inclination to separate is usually pushed along by the changing relations between husband and wife. Despite the culturally constructed barricades between them, despite the lack of pillow talk, and the dearth of opportunities for confidences, the two characteristically grow together in affection and personal intimacy as the years pass. One need only see a wife bringing the mid-day meal to her husband working in the fields, watch them sitting together, or overhear them talking cozily about the day's events to know that they have surmounted the barricades and have created their private togetherness apart from the commonalty of the joint family.

As the bonds between husband and wife strengthen, those between brother and brother tend to weaken. It is not so much that one causes the other as that there is a sharpening of a built-in contradiction. Brothers are both equal and unequal. They are unequal as elder and younger, but are equal in that each gets his equal share by Hindu law and South Asian Muslim tradition when they divide the joint family property.

Further, many men are restive as subordinates in a fraternal relationship. Though all share the belief that most human relations are hierarchical, each wants to take the dominant part in his own close encounters when he senses that he can do so (cf. Pettigrew 1975:57). As a younger brother gains some social standing on his own, he tends to feel himself to be more of an equal partner in the family enterprise. So an elder brother typically comes to find the younger increasingly willful and the younger finds the elder overbearingly domineering.

At this juncture each brother is likely also to take his wife's complaints more seriously than before. Many men feel caught in an uncomfortable bind, entangled in the tension between mother and wife. Subordinate though she is formally, his wife usually manages to let him know that she is being treated unfairly. She does not challenge the requirements of her role. What a daughter-in-law commonly does challenge are the unjust burdens and slights that she feels others in the joint family are placing on her.

So eventually the husband decides to split; about the time he does, his brothers may well be of a similar mind. In poor, landless families, this entails only the simple division of family effects and moving out. It is likely to occur not long after a bride has been brought in, perhaps while other brothers are still unmarried. But in families with land and valuables, the brothers must take the necessary legal steps to divide their common property. House, land, implements, and utensils, down to the last bag of salt, are apportioned. Each brother then lives separately with his wife and children; the cycle of family development begins anew. A nuclear

*A senior woman may wield much influence, though
it is rarely exerted openly, publicly, or directly.*

family becomes joint when a son marries and brings his bride into
the household. With her coming, the choreography of distancing
by a daughter-in-law begins again, part etiquette, part ritual, and
part defense and self-defense.

Wives are thus seen as both guarantors and disrupters of family
and patrilineage. Their fertility produces the blessings of children
and the blessed continuity of patriline. But fertility has to be de-
coupled from sex. A woman's sexuality is suspect because, for one
reason, it may be a means by which she can entice her husband
away from unswerving allegiance to parents and brothers. The potential of sex to impart shame is abated by such devices as the sepa-
rateness of wife and husband in public and by the hurried, almost
clandestine visitations for intercourse. Female sexuality also in-

volves menstruation, a polluting state (as childbirth is also) during which a woman must observe an intensified degree of seclusion so as to shield others from the ritual dangers of contact with her (cf. Jeffery 1979:110–12; Nath 1981:19; Krygier 1982:76–97).

Older women may wield much influence, as mothers and mothers-in-law, in their family's business affairs and sometimes even in their community's decisions. But they rarely exert that influence openly, publicly, or directly. Occasionally, men do acknowledge the realities of a senior woman's political capacity, as is testified by the examples of eminent women leaders from the Rani of Jhansi to Indira Gandhi.

While people readily tell that restraints on women serve to protect the women outside the home and to protect family cohesion within it, both functions also protect the men. A man, too, is socially vulnerable. Should a woman of his family be degraded by outsiders, he feels himself disgraced, his honor defiled. Should his joint family come under scorn as an arena of female discord and discredit, he and his close kinsmen feel under contempt and honor diminished. An ambitious man strives to build his honor through industry, loyalty, duty, judgment, and craft. However successful he may be in this, a critical cachet of his achievement is won through the marriage of his daughters into suitably high-ranking families. Conversely, the long building of his honor can come to grief if the women of his family fail him. Honor is the key good for these men, and their honor is balanced on the heads of the women.

CHAPTER 2

Purdah-Izzat and Variations

Izzat (an Arabic and Persian word) is the term for which "honor" is the usual translation. It is a word often heard in men's talk, particularly when the talk is about conflict, rivalry, and struggle. It crops up as a kind of final explanation for motivation, whether for acts of aggression or beneficence. It expresses a salient theme and includes some of the most highly valued purposes of a person's life. For the Pukhtun of Swat in northern Pakistan, their code of honor "is everything." For the Pirzada of Delhi, it is described as being their central concern (Lindholm 1982:189; Jeffery 1978:99–100).

Like any term of strong emotional resonance, it is used in various overlapping meanings and with many nuances. But it always refers to how a person carries out the group's values, how he or she realizes them in actual behavior. For Jat Sikhs in the Punjab, Joyce Pettigrew writes that their concept of izzat is a complex of values; it is a philosophy of life that includes their paramount concerns with power, with reciprocity in giving, equality in vengeance, and nonsubmission to threat. A family's izzat must be preserved at all costs and increased whenever possible. And "if the honor of a family's women is lost, so also is the family's entire public position" (1975:51, 58–59).

Public positions are the province of men, and so the primary referents of izzat are men. While a man's izzat is assessed by his kith and kin on several scores, the conduct of a family's women is always a cardinal consideration. Women are said to bear izzat also, as when it was remarked in a Himachal Pradesh village that it is bad for a woman's izzat if she does ploughing. But two women of that village were in an "uncertain moral position" because each had become economically independent of her husband. "The honour of her family depends on her behaviour; but if she cuts herself off from them she has no honour of her own" (Sharma 1980:91, 162).

Izzat can be a corporate or a personal attribute or both. Since a person's behavior in the community is commonly seen as a reflection of group traits rather than the isolable acts of an autonomous individual, izzat looms as a group and especially a family quality. Hence each woman's observance or nonobservance of her group's standards of purdah affects the izzat of all in her marital family, and not of them only. Should she grossly violate those standards, the izzat of her natal family will be hurt as well. A bride may be reminded by her parents that if she does not behave properly in her new home, her notoriety will damage the marriage chances of her still unmarried sisters and so may diminish their whole lives. Conversely, the reputation of both families will be enhanced if her conduct is devoted, dutiful, and irreproachable.

Izzat, then, takes in the zealously sought qualities of prestige and status, rank and esteem, respect and self-respect.* Shame (*sharm*) is the antithesis of izzat, to be avoided as diligently as izzat is sought. The term is also used often with positive connotation, as when a little boy is praised for having enough sensibility of shame to avoid the women's quarters (cf. Jeffery 1979:104).

The kind of izzat open to a person and family depends on their

---

* The nature of izzat as self-respect is illustrated by an incident among the Qalander, nomadic gypsylike entertainers of Pakistan. The most difficult and dangerous of their performances is with a bear. On one occasion a four-year-old boy, Raja, was working with his father and a large bear. At the moment when the child placed his head in the bear's mouth, the bear, startled by someone in the audience, lacerated the boy's neck and broke his leg. On the following morning, the act was repeated before the Qalander camp. The boy limped up and put his head in the bear's mouth. "At the successful conclusion he was loudly praised by those present, who concurred that both Raja and the bear had salvaged their self-respect (*izzat*) and could work effectively together" (Berland 1982:99–100).

social position. A family of a generally poor, low-ranking group can scarcely aspire to the izzat attainable by a family rich in land and proud of inherited status. But there are families of greater and lesser izzat within each set; a family of a lowly group may gain high regard both among its peers and more widely in its locality; one of high caste rank may come to be disdained by all.

Izzat and the dangers to it are judged in relative perspective. Zarina Bhatty tells of a Muslim family in a village of the Lucknow area. Its elders had long debated whether an unmarried daughter should be allowed to take a post as teacher in the village school. At the same time, they were proud that a woman of the family had been elected to the U. P. Legislative Assembly and had become a Minister in the State cabinet. Her political activities required her to mingle with many kinds of people and to be exposed to public gaze. "Such exposure was tolerated because to be a member of the State Assembly carries high prestige, but similar exposure in the midst of the village folk at the relatively low prestige level of a school teacher was clearly undesirable" (Bhatty 1975:32).

Izzat is best promoted by broadly based, desirable achievements, such as tangible wealth, unimpeachable piety, success in competition, the besting of one's enemies, the retention of followers and dependents, the skillful managing of allies, the tactful distribution of gifts and, critically, the conduct of the women of the family. Local public opinion is the gauge of a family's izzat. It is the general perception of a family's worth held by kinsmen, neighbors, and others in its social networks. That opinion is rarely unanimous in judgment, is often volatile in ratings, usually varies among local groups but it is nonetheless a force that affects much of a person's and family's striving.

A person and a family who gain high izzat in their community thereby command influence there. Thus izzat is a symbolic summary of past achievements and a main element in present power. Power, properly deployed, enhances izzat: izzat legitimates power.

While the family is the primary vessel of izzat, broader groups are also involved. An individual's serious failing may tarnish, or a notable achievement burnish, the izzat of all in the lineage, jati, or village (cf. Naveed-I-Rahat 1981:75). These are the wider circles with which a person identifies or is identified, in which he or she actually participates or may potentially participate. A person's grand achievements are likely to be paraded by members of his or her wider groups to enhance their own izzat.

Another dimension of izzat is more internal to the individual. Clues to it emerge when a man talks about how he has made (or will make) a good name for himself that will be long remembered. And a villager's typical desire to have several sons who are strong, good, and grown, stems not only from the material and political benefits they bring to him but also from the satisfaction of knowing that his name and the memory of him will last for at least another generation after his demise. So a man's drive to achieve a good name and a high degree of izzat is also a means of coping with the thoughts of one's passing. Together with religious acts, it is a way of overcoming oblivion, of defeating death.

The achievements open to a woman are mainly in raising a large set of vigorous, united, dutiful, children. In earlier times, a Hindu widow of some castes who committed *sati*, self-immolation on the funeral pyre of her husband, elevated the izzat of her family and lineage. A Muslim woman who, in the company of husband or son, completed the then perilous pilgrimage to Mecca, accrued izzat. Nowadays, less fiery and perilous lift can be imparted by a woman who, say, earns a medical degree or wins a post in the higher echelons of government service.

Izzat also devolves from distinguished ancestry. But if those who claim ancestral glories are to benefit, they must live up to them. If a group's inherited izzat is to count for much on the ground, its members must strive to uphold it. Izzat does not keep well; it has to be continually reaffirmed in practice, reinforced in action, defended against challenge, and rewon and advanced in competition.

Ancestral memories are predominantly about males, and genealogy is usually reckoned through males only. Yet family izzat is not only pivotally dependent on the conduct of the wives, but also that izzat is inevitably tested when the marriage of a daughter is arranged.

In negotiating a marriage, each side carefully considers the izzat of the other family, the amount of the dowry and other material transactions, as well as the personal qualities of the prospective spouse. Each family ponders on how these ratings will affect their own standing and so influence the prospects of any unmarried daughters and sons. Among Hindus, the family that gives the bride is the defined inferior in the transaction; a bridegroom can be married to a spouse of somewhat lower standing than his without loss of family face. Not so for the bride and her family. They must, to preserve or increase family izzat, secure a bridegroom of as high a personal and family position, within the caste span of possible spouses, as their own resources and reputation can provide.

Each of the families linked by the transfer of a daughter and the acquisition of a bride expects to gain from the affiliation and usually does. Each tends to support the other in political and material ways unless contrary circumstances arise. Thus if a Bangladesh villager is to enhance his *ijjat* (the Bengali word for izzat), "it is required for him to have a network of . . . powerful affinal relatives" (Aziz 1979:42). Among Jat Sikh families on the other side of the subcontinent, the ties formed through a marriage "connected families otherwise isolated and placed a whole network of links at the disposal of each of the members" (Pettigrew 1975:56).

A brother who gives freely and lavishly to a married sister and her children gains in local esteem (cf. Eglar 1960:99). Gift-giving is, in general, an important means of accruing izzat, especially when the gifts are made generously, judiciously, and publicly. Those to a married sister and her children are among the more meritorious of presentations.

Izzat is mainly positive in connotation; it embraces what a man should do if he can. Purdah is more negative; it covers what a woman might do but should not. There is some feedback between a family's izzat and its purdah practices. The practices, properly done, enhance the izzat. The izzat, to be properly maintained, requires unfailing purdah observance. So purdah strengthens izzat as izzat strengthens purdah.

VARIATIONS: AGE, REGION, CLASS, AND EDUCATION

Within these broad patterns of purdah there are regular variations. One variation is by age, another by linguistic-cultural region, a third by economic class and educational level.

Age is always a factor because purdah is a cultural attribute of women rather than of females. Before her puberty, a girl does not have to guard her movements and signal her deference as she does after puberty. True, she is taught from early childhood that she must sit differently, behave differently, carry different responsibilities than do the boys, but a Muslim girl does not assume the full mantle of purdah until she is nubile, and a Hindu girl not until she is married.

Later in her life and particularly as she becomes busy with caring for her growing children, she can gradually ease the stringency of some of the purdah practices she should follow as a young wife. She begins to move about outside more, perhaps to do a bit of shopping or expand her visits to women of other households. As an elder matron, she can have still more leeway. But, as we have noted, some proprieties are not abandoned. Even an elderly matron will cover her face and fall silent before her husband's father so long as they both shall live. Nor does passing through her menopause permit a woman to pass insouciantly through town and village streets (cf. Vreede-de Stuers 1968:82; Sharma 1980:46; Pastner 1974:410, 1982:173; Luschinsky 1962:341; Jacobson 1982:90, 95).

Purdah practices also vary by linguistic-cultural region. Ahmad points out how Muslim as well as Hindu family and kinship relations differ in different "regional cultural environments" (1976b: xxiv–xxx). For the Punjab, Joyce Pettigrew notes that Punjabi-speaking Sikhs, Hindus, and Muslims have quite similar cultures in fundamental respects, including relations between the sexes (1975:4).

The Punjab and the other regions of the subcontinent are better

A village daughter carries water home.

*Many daughters and daughters-in-law go to the well
daily to bring home water for their families.*

defined in terms of core social-cultural and linguistic characteristics than by neatly drawn map perimeters that demarcate what
are usually mixed, transitional border territories (cf. Sopher 1980:
290–93). In a later discussion we compare the northern subcontinent as a world area with other world areas including Southeast
Asia, the Middle East, and North Africa.

There are gradients by region in the strength of the purdah-izzat
complex. It is upheld most stringently and zealously among the
peoples of the northwestern sector of the subcontinent, through
the middle Ganges basin and Bangladesh. The purdah zone thus
comprises all of Pakistan and Bangladesh, plus the Indian states
(each roughly a linguistic-cultural region) of Punjab, Rajasthan,
Haryana, Uttar Pradesh, together with adjoining parts of Madhya
Pradesh, Kashmir, and Himachal Pradesh.

Purdah is much less compelling among Hindus of Bihar and West Bengal but is strongly sustained among Bangladeshis. It is given greatest weight among those Hindus who are most dedicated to the Rajput-Kshatriya model. By contrast, those Hindus who follow the Brahmanic model of eternal vigilance about ritual purity and pollution are generally less worried about the danger to men's honor and the disruption of men's polity by women. There is much less veiling and less rigid seclusion among the Dravidian-speaking peoples of the south. Not that the relations between men and women in South India are utterly different from those in the north, rather that the emphases are differently placed, fears and rectitudes differently arranged.

This is well shown in Pauline Kolenda's insightful comparison of wedding rites that she has observed among Hindu villagers of the north and of the south of India. In the northern village of Khalapur, north of Delhi in Uttar Pradesh, she studied the Rajputs, the dominant caste in the village. The other village group is that of the Nattati Nadar of Kanyakumari District in southernmost Tamil Nadu.

Weddings present particularly good avenues for the study of gender relations, all the more so in South Asia where weddings are of great social and personal concern. Kolenda finds structural similarity in both sets of rites and suggests that the similarity stems from a common base in Sanskritic rites prescribed in Hindu scriptures (1984:104–105, 108–109).

There are also fundamental differences between the two which reflect divergent images of man, woman, and family. While the analysis is focused on the comparison between the Rajputs and Nadars of the respective localities, Kolenda indicates that the differences between them represent, at many points, the general differences in gender relations as between the Dravidian south and the north of India. Among the Rajputs, a bride is given as tribute by a subordinate family to a superior one. The act of being bride-givers makes the one family ipso facto the inferior of the family that receives the bride. That formal inferiority is made manifest through the wedding ritual and long after, when the woman's family is obliged to make periodic gifts to the husband and his family. The bride-receivers are under no obligation to reciprocate (Kolenda 1984:108, 111).

The Rajput wedding ceremony includes several dramatizations of antagonism between the two families and the trauma of separation felt by the bride and her family. The Nadar rites invoke no such antagonism or trauma, their emphasis is instead on easing the new union and fostering the fertility, the "blossoming," of the woman. Thus at one juncture in the ceremony, the Rajput bridegroom is "teased unmercifully" by the bride's female relatives but a Nadar groom at a similar juncture is "treated respectfully and affectionately" by female kin of the bride (ibid., 110).

When a Rajput bride leaves the house to be taken to her new household, she weeps copiously, with both ritual and real sorrow. The women of her natal family weep and wail with her. Such weeping is repeated whenever her brother or father comes to escort her back to her childhood home. Arriving there, "she weeps ritually on her mother's shoulder, chanting the misery of her separation and recalling their mutual sorrows" (ibid., 111). No such display of sorrow is required of a Nadar woman.

When the Rajput bride arrives at her husband's home, the sisters of the bridegroom bar her entrance. The groom then presents each of them with a gift, buying off their opposition as it were, and the bride is then permitted to enter. Among the Nadar, the sisters of the groom, far from opposing the bride's coming, play an important part in the formal welcoming and preparation of the bride. They help place the *tali* around the bride's neck; it is the prime material symbol of the union.

In both communities, a girl is given a series of pre-nuptial baths. The Nadar explain this as a special cleansing of her menstrual pollution. The Rajputs say that these baths symbolically terminate the bride's virginity as necessary preparation for the physical termination to follow. Pollution and purity are subsidiary matters in the Rajput rites, cardinal considerations for the Nadar (ibid., 109).

A difference in substance as well as in symbol is that an affluent Nadar family may give a house and paddy fields to their daughter

at her marriage. These are deeded to her and are in her own name
(ibid., 108, 111). The dowry that is transferred at the marriage of a
Rajput girl belongs to the groom and his family, decidedly not to
her personally. A bridegroom's family in the north would scarcely
allow a young wife to be endowed with such property of her own
lest it increase her power and independence.

Further, the parents of a Nadar bride may induce the groom to
live with or near them. Later, they themselves may move to be
close to the couple. Rajputs and other northern groups, by contrast,
consider it shameful for a man to live with his affines. A wife's
close kin must be kept at a social and usually physical distance
from her married household. Her mother is never expected to visit
her there. When her father or brother comes to escort her back to
their place, they should not accept hospitality from her husband's
family. If they have a meal there, they should pay for it (ibid., 111–
12). Nadars have no such separation. The bride's mother, indeed,
goes to inspect the couple's new home on the evening after the
wedding (ibid., 111).

The inherent antagonism ascribed by Rajputs to families linked
through marriage is one reason given for village exogamy. "Of
course, we would not marry among ourselves," a Rajput told
Kolenda. It is as though a marriage that was close in kinship or
in space would be blighted. It would muddle the subordination
of a wife if she was also a kinswoman and was not cut off from
her natural allies. The Nadars see less threat in a new wife. Their
concerns are, quite conversely, with strengthening the family by
the inclusion of a bride already related. "Of course, if we can, we
marry within the family," a Nadar explained, meaning kindred or
extended family. The preference in the south is that the children of
a brother and sister be united in marriage (ibid., 111–12). Muslims
also prefer close-in marriages, as we shall discuss later, though
their prime preference is a union between the children of brothers,
a union forbidden among Hindus of the south.

In this contrastive perspective, we can detect again the appre-
hensions about an incoming wife felt by Hindu family elders in

the north. Such fears do not grip family elders of the Dravidian-speaking south. Elders in the northern zone seem to be perpetually on guard lest the power of a junior wife—subordinated, submissive, self-effacing though she must appear—be yet strong enough to subvert the precious but frangible bonds among the family's men. Wedding rites in the Hindu South, Kolenda points out, celebrate "female fertility and close-knit connubia," those of the North emphasize "hierarchical prestige relations" of men (ibid., 114).

Another comparison of gender relations as between southern and northern India is sketched by Susan S. Wadley in the summarizing chapter of a volume of studies entitled *The Powers of Tamil Women* (1980). Wadley's analysis touches on a broader range of topics, rites, and regions than does Kolenda's; it presents much the same findings. Wadley's analysis, too, highlights the relatively advantaged status held by a Tamil woman as against her North Indian counterpart.

As a bride she comes into her new family as a familiar relative, or at least as a known welcomed person. By contrast, the Hindu bride of the North is confronted by a set of strangers, sometimes doubting, or even downright hostile. In South India, the design of the rituals and the ambiance of the wedding aim to enhance the bride's present well-being and her future fertility. We should emphasize that such considerations are not entirely absent from northern Hindu weddings. Welcome and affection are also shown to her, but these ceremonies bear the added brunt of the domination-subordination consideration which preoccupy a man's continual strain for honor and prestige.

In other rituals as well, a Tamil woman appears as a less vulnerable, better endowed person than a Hindu woman of the North appears to be in similar rites. There are, for example, rituals in both North and South in which a woman reaffirms and reinforces her bonds with her brothers, Wadley notes, basing her comments on a study by Holly B. Reynolds, in the same volume. In these rites a northern woman seeks to renew and strengthen the protection she may expect from her brothers. The southern rite emphasizes the prosperity which she may bring to them. Their future prosperities may be intertwined since the son of one is the preferred spouse for the daughter of the other (Wadley 1980:161–64).

Female puberty rites, Wadley continues (ibid., 164) are commonly celebrated among South Indians, often with considerable ostentation as indices for prestige. Among the people of North India such rites are virtually absent, even the event of a girl's first menstruation may be hushed up. The reason for this difference, Wadley suggests, is that menarche is a clear sign of a female's sexuality and impending fertility, and since her fertility potential is greatly and openly valued, the event should be celebrated with public acclaim. Moreover, sexuality brings on dangers, both natural and supernatural, which must be controlled, cooled, and managed through the rituals for the occasion.

Why then, should there be such major differences in sex roles and relations as between Hindu South and Hindu North? (Muslims, as we shall note, present still other differences in these matters.) One fundamental economic factor is suggested by Wadley, and we shall take notice of it again later. It is that women's work contribution to the staple crop, rice, in the south is proportionately much greater than are the inputs from women's work to the growing of the staple northern crop, wheat.

Seen in a long time perspective, say of the past millennium, those who followed the North Indian system of gender may have been advantaged under conditions of constant and imminent fighting, exacerbated by lack of effective central authority. Threatened with incursions by outsiders, a band of brothers could quickly rally in defense or strike out in offense. Brothers-in-arms could readily be recruited from among co-religionists or caste fellows. They would be relatively unencumbered by ties to or responsibilities for females and affines. People who followed the South Indian system would gain productive, economic advantages, rather than military ones. Their central unit was not the band of brothers but rather what Wadley, citing Brenda Beck, calls the kin nucleus of the "female surrounded by father, brothers, husband and sons" (ibid., 161). They could rely on a compact group of kin-linked workers to plant and harvest the paddy. This led to greatly increased wealth and power for those who owned landed property. That wealth, in turn, was often expanded to increase religious as well as social power by elaborate measures and rites to avoid pollution and enhance purity.

This comparison stresses the differences that exist atop the common cultural base. Another kind of comparison, made by Ursula Sharma of Hindu villagers in the two adjoining northern region-states of Punjab and Himachal Pradesh, brings out the common cultural stratum that underlies differences in gender relations.

The Punjabi women are personally more open and assertive, though more housebound and more restricted in public. Himachali women are more reserved at all times and less obliged to refer their actions constantly to the men. Yet, "whilst these differences were experienced as very important, when it came to analysis they were less significant than they seemed." In both regions, "there is a fund of common norms and images which all the women I studied recognized as bearing on their lives, a warp of common values regarding women's social role which underlies all the differences due to class and regional culture" (ibid., 195, 197). These norms, images, and values are also shared among many other people across the northern reaches of the subcontinent. Such widely shared ideas and practices concerning gender should be documented in further studies. They came about partly because of a common scriptural base, as Kolenda has noted for Hindu wedding rites, and also rise from the large, ancient ambit of Indian civilization as a whole.

Thus in E. V. Daniel's study, *Fluid Signs: Being a Person the Tamil Way* (1984), a reader alert to pan-civilizational patterns can find numerous parallels to northern gender concepts. In the chapter on sexuality, Daniel discusses many ideas that are also held by northerners, among them the dangers to men from sexual intercourse, the metaphor of the field (woman) and the seed (man), and the importance of balance in bodily substances, particularly sexual secretions (Daniel 1984:163–81). Some of these concepts are indeed held by peoples far beyond South Asia, but within the subcontinent, both southerners and northerners phrase them in a

particularly Indic way. That is also true among the Tamils and Sin-
halese of Sri Lanka as can be seen in Obeyesekere's penetrating
account of the cult of the goddess Pattini (1984:451–82 *passim*).

Variations in purdah by economic class are everywhere readily
apparent. Women of the poorer strata, mainly of the groups lowest
in a local social hierarchy, are more visible publicly than are those
of wealthier higher-ranking families. They can be seen working in
the fields, dickering in the bazaar, peddling bangles and women's
needs from courtyard to courtyard, and as servants in the richer
homes (cf. Jacobson 1976a:196–97; 1982:94; Sharma 1978:225).
Poor women, too, cover their faces before the male elders inside
their households and before elder males of the village. But they
tend to relax the in-house gestures soon after marriage, and generally display them with less meticulous urgency. In their work outside, they encounter more men than do the more strictly secluded
women, yet a senior man, at least a considerate one, is likely to
advance some warning note when he approaches women laborers
at work, quite as he does for the women in his own home.

While poorer women go out more often and go farther afield,
their movements are still within close bounds. No women may sit
with the clusters of men when they gather in the evening to smoke
and talk. The poorest woman is not likely to stroll alone at night
through the streets. And even in homes where hunger presses, a
woman does not eat until the men have finished.

Those women of the lower and poorer groups who receive wages
for their own work are likely to have more personal independence than do women without such income. Divorce and remarriage are usually possible for Hindu women of the lower castes
and are strongly disapproved or entirely forbidden in the higher
castes. Widows in the low-ranking groups may remarry; those of
the Hindu higher echelons may not.

The poor hold to the common values concerning purdah, but
they cannot afford the costs of more stringent observances. The
secluding of a family's women requires some surplus of family
income. Thus among the Rajputs of Khalapur, most men want to
have their wives in purdah, "although it is a luxury, since to do

this the men must do without their help in the fields and hire servants to help them in the house" (Minturn and Hitchcock 1966: 34). When a poor family becomes affluent enough to adopt more rigorous purdah, its women are generally eager to do so. They may still do much hard work inside the home, but increased seclusion for them means greater freedom from grinding labor in the fields or unpleasant toil as house servants (cf. Vreede-de Stuers 1968: 82–83; Jeffery 1978:174).

At first the women may withdraw only from certain kinds of work, then with increasing prosperity increase their purdah seclusion. How much outside work a woman may do without damage to her family's image and self-image varies by caste and occupational group. But whatever the local standards may be, strict purdah observances are prestigious, provide an important credit to family izzat, are at once a signal of family fortune, and, for the upwardly mobile, a sign of realized aspiration (cf. A. F. A. Husain 1958:96; Papanek 1982 [1973]:42–43 [322–23]; Luschinsky 1962:338, 380–81; Brijbhushan 1980:21; Pastner 1982:173–76; Jacobson 1976a: 209; Sharma 1980:116–23; Bhatty 1975:30).

Intensifying their purdah practices is not the only elevating change made by rising families, though it is one of the most important steps. They may also revise their previous ritual procedures, their diet, their marriage practices, their exchanges of goods and services, and their group name. These changes are part of the regular process of social mobility that has been termed Sanskritization or Rajputization for Hindus, with a corresponding process of Islamization or Ashrafization among Muslims. A family that accomplishes this process raises its standing within its endogamous group and in its locality. When a large set of intermarrying families do so in the same degree and during the same period of time, they can lift the ranking of their whole group (cf. Ahmad 1976b:xxx–xxxii; Mandelbaum 1970:427–520).

To this traditional process, another phase has been added, one which includes the education of girls and the consequent shift in their practice of purdah as women. As a family prospers and increases the seclusion of its women, it characteristically also extends the education of its children. Education is necessary equipment for better livelihood and further social mobility. At first, it is the family's sons who are given whatever education is attainable and feasible. But soon the daughters are allowed to attend school longer because an educated boy and his family require that a prospective bride have an education comparable (but preferably not equal) to his own. So daughters must be given enough education to assure and advance the family's position. In cities and towns, a small but increasing proportion of educated women do take jobs, as teachers, health professionals, office workers, and government servants (cf. Vatuk 1972:27–29; Beech 1982:124–25). Such employment does not usually damage their family's standing, their own marriage chances, or their reputations after marriage. The income they bring in does much to assuage any blemish caused by their daily excursions outside the household.

A woman with a high school or college education is likely to be less stringent in her purdah observance and to have less stringency expected of her than is true for women of the same economic class and region who have little education. This is partly because years of school attendance accustom a girl to being out of the house independently, partly because she is typically older and less dependent psychologically when she joins her conjugal household, partly because the family elders, perhaps grudgingly or unconsciously, make allowance for her educational accomplishments. That they allowed her to attend high school or college is, in itself, an indication of her family's flexibility.

Purdah tends to be more strictly practiced in villages now than in towns. There are noteworthy exceptions such as the Pirzada of Delhi whose occupation as keepers of a Muslim shrine requires strict orthodoxy, including stringent observance of purdah (cf. Jeffery 1979). One reason for somewhat less close seclusion in towns and cities is the greater incidence of girls' education there. Another is the more limited space in town dwellings. Doranne Jacobson recounts that a woman from a village in Madhya Pradesh who was married into a town family said that some of her husband's relatives would laugh at her if she were to cover her face completely before them. Conversely, when a city-bred wife visited her village relatives, she did not veil before a man who was her classificatory elder brother-in-law. He responded uncritically, "City girls don't cover their faces."

The villagers know about the relaxed town customs, but they consider most urban behavior irrelevant to their own lives. "The man who accepted his city-born sister-in-law's unveiled face would consider such behavior in his own wife to be shameless and brazen." It so happens that the wealthier Muslims of this village have dramatically decreased their observance of purdah but the other villagers had not been affected, at the time of the study, by their example (Jacobson 1976a:197, 1982:104–5).

Rising families make other changes in their life-style, as we have mentioned, but purdah shifts are particularly noted and notable. They are an important part of the double movement by which materially successful groups of the lower echelons of a local hierarchy adopt traditionally prestigious practices. At the same time those of the higher echelons are dropping some of these customs and taking on others of a modern cachet (cf. Bhatty 1975:31–34; Mandelbaum 1970:464–67).

Although purdah practices are indeed being changed among urban, educated women, they are not totally discarded nor have the underlying values been jettisoned. Two studies of urban Hindu families, one done by Sylvia Vatuk in Meerut (1972), the other by Mary H. Beech in Calcutta (1982), show that some of the practices and the concepts supporting them are still viable in an urban setting.

Two adjacent neighborhoods (*mohalla*) in the city of Meerut, forty miles northeast of Delhi, were the scene of Vatuk's observations. Both are relatively new subdivisions and the residents are largely middle-class people, employed in white-collar jobs made possible for them by their education. Their patterns of consumption and style of life differ from those carried on in the mohallas of the old city whose residents are, in the main, poorer and with less education. Kinship organization in the old mohallas "still resembles that of the rural districts in all important respects" (Vatuk

1972:190–91). But in the new neighborhoods most of the men have achieved occupational mobility and that often requires geographical mobility. Many have come from rural places or other towns to work in the city and, after marriage, do not live with their parents or other kin.

Such neolocal residence is an important differential because those of the younger married women who do live with parents-in-law keep seclusion as they would in the village, "perhaps even more so because one need not leave the urban house to perform natural functions or do chores." They go out of the neighborhood only occasionally. When they are outdoors within their own neighborhood they must veil as completely as village women do in the locality of their married residence. But as soon as these Meerut women leave their own neighborhood they unveil and only cover the top of the head with the edge of the sari as practically all women do (ibid., 119).

Within the home, a woman who lives with parents-in-law veils before senior males and before her husband when others are present, quite in the village pattern. In some households, the father-in-law, especially if he is educated and the mother-in-law has died, will encourage the daughter-in-law to stop veiling to him. He does this partly because it is inconvenient for a man, in the narrower living spaces of the city, to keep out of the way of women who should avoid him. His education also plays a part, for in-house purdah "is one of the traditional practices most often attacked by educated men, although heatedly defended by older women" (ibid., 1972:120).

For a married woman who lives separately with her husband and children, far from her husband's parents and elder brothers, purdah restrictions within the home are not necessary and are observed only when receiving male visitors. Such a woman spends much more time with her children than she would in a village joint family and she has greater responsibility for supervising the children's education (cf. Seymour 1975). A father, too, interacts with his children more, without the constraints about doing so in the presence of his parents.

Although husband and wife have much more personal independence in these Meerut families, they still uphold certain of the traditional values about marital relations. "Even in the urban nuclear household, the husband is expected to be the dominant partner, responsible for handling outside affairs and for making major decisions for household members. The wife is ideally submissive" (Vatuk 1972:123). In some of these families the wife does, in fact, dominate the husband but, as in the village, "it is not a publicly overt dominance." Most women of these white-collar neighborhoods continue to make the traditional obeisance of touching the husband's feet on rising in the morning (ibid., 124, 126).

A woman who does not formally avoid her father-in-law and elder brother-in-law still is not likely to talk with them freely or casually. When she does discuss some household matter with them, her eyes are downcast, her head is well-covered, her voice is low. "An attitude of respectful deference from the daughter-in-law is considered particularly important if the traditional avoidance customs have been abandoned, because showing respect is the manifest function of purdah observance" (ibid., 120).

Urban people usually want to keep alive their bonds with village relatives. If they can maintain their legal interest in joint family property, they do so. The common causes of friction and family fission no longer apply when some members of a village joint family live in a city. The city members like, as Vatuk puts it, to remain structurally as close as feasible though spatially distant. And the relations between a city woman and her father-in-law remain structurally apart even though they may be spatially close (ibid., 135, 194).

People in these mohallas form social ties with neighbors with whom they have some previous connection by kinship, or acquaintance, or common geographic-cultural origin. Kinship terms are commonly used for the neighbors with whom one is friendly. In selecting social intimates, a couple prefers to associate with the wife's natal kin rather than with the husband's because of the traditional double standard of behavior for "daughter" and "bride." These city women still feel under constraint with husband's kin,

Men have their own social networks.

particularly those senior in age to him, and are much more at ease with their own natal kin (ibid., 138, 168, 195).

As in a village, men have different social networks and meeting places than do women. Men spend their free time with work colleagues, friends, and kinsmen. They meet in teashops, coffee houses, or restaurants. When a man visits the home of a friend or kinsman he rarely takes his wife along. He and his host stay in the sitting-room, the housewife rarely joins them, and she sends in refreshments with a child. A woman has her own network of kin and friendly neighbors and visits with them in the early afternoon. In this city setting as in a village, a woman "who never leaves her house" is praised. Here as in other urban places, husbands and wives are beginning to spend more time together and the better-educated women are able to move about much more freely than traditional conventions and neighborhood gossip would otherwise allow (Vatuk 1972:124–26).

The middle-class women studied by Mary H. Beech in Calcutta have similarly modified some purdah practices and have retained others. They, too, show respect before the husband's father, his elder brothers, and other family elders. In their presence, a woman of this Hindu sample covers her face or at least her head with the end of her sari, lowers her gaze, restricts her conversation, and avoids talk with her husband in their hearing (Beech 1982:116–23).

These women go out of the house a good deal. They ride buses and trains to visit, to worship, to take children to school. They do some shopping occasionally, but in most households a man continues to do the daily marketing. Those women who are employed in jobs where they work along with men gave Beech various rationalizations for their situation. One was that there were exceptional or emergency circumstances in their family; another was to suggest that the workplace is really a kind of extended household. More loftily, some emphasized the potential of their common humanity above the proprieties of their feminity (ibid., 129–34). These employed, educated women still feel it necessary to explain, perhaps to themselves as much as to others, their breach of traditional constraints.

Observations of educated Muslim women in cities, comparable to the studies of Hindu women in Meerut and Calcutta, are not yet available. But there are indications that educated Muslim women similarly modify some purdah practices and retain basic concepts about womanly conduct (cf. Roy 1979:69, 123).

In all, studies of the educated urban middle class (perhaps numerically the largest national middle class in the world) indicate that among most of them the traditional demure behavior and other purdah values are still well regarded. To explore why purdah seems so firmly embedded in psyche and culture and why so many continue to uphold the values and follow the customs relating to purdah, we next consider some of the effects of purdah practice on personality and society.

CHAPTER 3

Personality and Childhood

A woman's personality typically matures and functions within a much narrower sphere than does a man's—more restricted in space, in activities, in social relations, in opportunities for self-assertion, power, and control. As we have noted, women are expected to be dependent on men in almost all domains and periods of life. Do they, therefore, develop dependent personalities?

Men are the owners of the land and of all productive resources; they conduct all outside transactions; only males perform the principal public ceremonies and participate in public discussions. Within the household, a woman must ordinarily have the permission of the man or men to make any significant change or decision.

A bride's passage from girl to married woman is culturally posted as being a difficult one. The wedding songs and pre-wedding talk anticipate her plight in her new home. When she is finally taken away, the tears and sobs (sometimes wails and flailings) of the dear ones whom she is leaving dramatize the sad separation. In her new home, she is confronted with an array of strange people, new responsibilities, and different relationships. While a Muslim bride may transfer to another household within the same community where her new family are not strangers, she is nonetheless shifted, as Patricia Jeffery writes of the Muslim Pirzada of Delhi, from the calm life of beloved daughter to the harassed existence of the new wife (1979:120). Her state of mind is not eased if she thinks, as young girls tend to do in the villages studied by Ursula Sharma, that she has been a burden on her parents, all the more because they have spent so much, perhaps their entire savings, on her marriage (Sharma 1980:174; Nath 1981:19).

A woman owns, in her own right, only the jewelry she has been given, mainly by her natal family, at her marriage and on subsequent occasions. These should not be taken from her without her consent even though all property is in some sense considered a family resource. But as a young wife, her control over these valuables may be precarious, subject to peremptory sale in a family emergency, or expropriated for a bride of her husband's kin, or lost through simple, inside theft. An older woman can usually dispose of her jewelry as she wishes (cf. Jacobson 1976b; Sharma 1980: 50–53; Luschinsky 1962:592).*

Muslim scriptural law stipulates that a bride receive a contractual settlement at her marriage, a deed of money, land, or other property that will be owed her if the marriage is ended through death or divorce. The setting of *mahr*, the dower, is part of Muslim marriage ceremonies, but in actuality very few wives ever claim their dower rights just as few Muslim or Hindu women lay claim to their legal rights of inheritance. Most Muslim brides receive a token payment and then formally renounce their claim to the *mahr* settlement (cf. Aziz 1979:213; D'Souza 1976:166–67; Jacobson 1976a:186, 207; Jeffery 1979:56; Lambert 1976:67; Lindholm 1982:140; Papanek 1982[1973]:24–25[307]). Among Muslims of the Ashraf classes in Delhi, Cora Vreede-de Stuers recorded only two instances in which the dower or part of it had been paid "in well over a hundred cases." But much importance attaches to setting a high dower, not for the woman's economic protection but because "the *mahr* is rather a sign of the constant preoccupation with family prestige (*izzat*)" (1968:14–15).

So the economic dependence of both Hindu and Muslim women on the men of their families is typically quite complete. There are exceptions. Occasionally, a widow with young children will work

---

* Doranne Jacobson tells that two important Muslim leaders could obtain a Western education only because the mother of each pawned her jewelry for the purpose (Jacobson 1976b:171, citing Minault 1973:6–8).

or manage the lands left by her husband, lest her sons be robbed of their patrimony. Women who work for pay in the fields or as house servants may have some say in the spending of their wages, although these are usually pooled in the family purse and the men have primary control of that (cf. Sharma 1980:206–8).

In her interpersonal relations also, a younger woman has little or no leeway for selecting her own friends and companions. Her everyday relations are mainly with the other women of the household and of the immediate neighborhood. If, as is common, her mother-in-law and her husband's brothers' wives live either in the same house or nearby, she must interact and cope with them continually. Villagers expect these women to quarrel and often enough they do. They are together through most of each day; quarters are usually cramped; petty annoyances abound, especially when heat and discomfort are high or when stocks of food and cooking fuel are low. Ordinarily, there are no deep-rooted bonds between the close-living sisters-in-law. Tensions between mother-in-law and daughters-in-law are celebrated in song, story, cinema, and from 1981 to 1984, in newspaper headlines about Indira Gandhi and her daughter-in-law, Maneka.

When grown brothers living together decide to partition their joint family, the blame, as we have noted, is usually laid to quarrels among the women (Jeffery 1979:168; Pastner 1974:412–13). Ursula Sharma points out that, in her observation, women's household quarrels occur more frequently than do those among men, in part because there are chronic causes of irritation which women are not in a position to resolve and which men will not help them resolve. Moreover, "brothers do quarrel but it is less acceptable for them to indulge in public slanging matches than it would be for their wives." Yet the actual relations among the women are often more complex than the villagers' stereotypes admit. A woman may well receive material and emotional support from her mother-in-law and sister-in-law and give needed support to them (Sharma 1980:178–85).

Nonetheless, the strains within the household commonly do weigh upon a woman. She looks, in the early years of her marriage, to her natal family for relief. She usually makes long visits to her natal home, if it is in another town or village, with her children. She and they enjoy a freer and more favored ambience there, away from the stricter discipline of their own home (Freed and Freed 1985:142–43). There, too, are her brothers, characteristically her principal allies and benefactors. They treat each of their beloved sister's children as individuals to be cherished rather than as role carriers to be socialized.

Women hold this relationship dear and so they are generally reluctant to endanger it by accepting their inheritance rights and sharing in the family property with their brothers. Muslim women have long been entitled to a share by scriptural law and Hindu women became so entitled by the Hindu Succession Act of 1956. Accepting inheritance rights might place a woman in rivalry with her brothers and the vast majority of women reject that prospect. It is mainly for this reason that most women resign their legal inheritance rights (cf. V. Das 1973:38–39; Naveed-I-Rahat 1981:76; Eglar 1960:97–98; Bertocci 1974:116; Sharma 1980:47–59; Jeffery 1979:56, 166; Rahman 1982:297–98).

Yet, as Ursula Sharma tells, the village women with whom she talked do not feel excluded from ownership of land. They speak of "my land" or "our land," although they have no legal control over it. They see it as family property, held in the name of the male head in behalf of all members of the family, female as well as male (Sharma 1980:53).

As mentioned earlier, with the years, a woman commonly comes to feel more secure in her marital family. She may be able to rally her husband, no longer a lad, to her aid or at least to engage his interest in her problems. Later still, she may enjoy the dutiful support of resident sons and visiting daughters. A fortunate woman may have helpful brothers, an understanding husband, supportive sons, a sympathetic mother-in-law, and compatible sisters-in-law. But even a woman who has all of them must still be expressedly and expressively subordinate to husband and family elders, precluded from any independent stance outside the domestic scene and, as a junior wife, have little independence within it.

Such conditions might be expected to make for impoverished and stunted personalities but, as some close observers attest, seems not to do so. "Paradoxically, despite their isolation and inferior status, women are much less conflicted than their husbands." This comes from Charles Lindholm about the Pukhtun of Swat in northern Pakistan (1982:191). While the Pukhtun, as we shall note later, differ considerably from Muslims of other South Asian regions, Pukhtun women are under equal or greater constraints. Hanna Papanek says of the city women she studied in Pakistan, "Despite the restrictions of the purdah system, at least some women show a greater degree of self-confidence than comparable middle-class men" (1982[1973]:33[314–15]).

In the concluding passage of her account of women in North and Central India, Doranne Jacobson writes that a woman may undergo much unhappiness and frustration. "But with rare exceptions, she has a clear sense of what she is and what she should be doing. In doing what is expected of her she feels a deep sense of achievement. Every woman complains, for to pride oneself in one's good fortune would be to tempt the fates, but few women would trade places with anyone else" (1977a:107). This conclusion comes out of long residence among and intimate conversations with village women. It is a considered distillation from experience, not derived from answers to quick survey questions.

Complaints were frequently heard by Sylvia Vatuk when she was studying older women in a village that has been encapsulated in the expansion of New Delhi. But there was a marked discrepancy between the voluble dissatisfactions and "the observed high level of good-humoured and extraordinarily active participation and interest in social, work, and family activities" (1975:151).

The dependence of women, Ursula Sharma found, is held by them to be a moral good. "There is a positive celebration of the dependence of women upon men, especially among the high-status groups" (1980:156). But this does not mean that these women are wanting in self-confidence; they "often showed great courage and determination in standing up for themselves in difficult circumstances" (ibid., 174). And while some would complain about their lot as landless laborers, or as housewives trying to make do during rapid inflation, few had any quarrel with traditional women's roles. "Most of the women I know did not experience their position *as women* as being oppressive ..." (ibid., 208). Similarly, the Pirzada Muslim women in Delhi, with whom Patricia Jeffery talked, poured out to her "a cascade of grievances" but they were about particular injustices and personal abuses rather than about the basic rules; "... they press for small changes which would make their position more palatable to them but which cannot be said to strike at the root of the *purdah* system" (1979:119, 170).

This is not to say that women never complain about women's place in society. "We women are the low caste," comments the central character in a documentary film about a village family in Haryana. It is to say that these women have been socialized into a hierarchical order of which a cardinal principle is the hierarchy of gender. The great majority of them have thoroughly internalized the norms of purdah (cf. Jacobson 1982:84).*

Many are aware that women of other life-styles, urban or educated or rich or foreign, follow other rules of conduct, but they generally consider those ways irrelevant to the realities of their own lives. Their daughters and grand-daughters who get a high school or college education tend to perceive those realities differently, to resent and work to discard some of the strictures but, as we have noted, they typically hold to certain basics of the traditional standards for womanly conduct.

There are active feminist organizations which have achieved notable successes, especially in getting legislation passed. Their

---

* Mrs. Meer Hassan Ali, an Englishwoman who lived at the court of Oudh from 1816 to 1828, wrote of the rigidly cloistered women of the nobility, "They are happy in their confinement; and never having felt the sweets of liberty, would not know how to use the boon if it were granted them" (1917[1832]: 167). Mrs. Ali repeatedly urges her English readers not to judge Indian Muslim customs by the standards of their own society, or to gauge a Muslim woman's unhappiness by how an Englishwoman might feel if she were placed in purdah.

members are largely urban and educated but with a growing presence among some village women (cf. Omvedt 1980).

A great source of comfort and pleasure for a young wife, as we have noted, is her visit to her childhood home. Women with young children are likely to spend weeks, even months of every year in their parents' household and village. Ursula Sharma tells how, in the Hindu villages she studied, a young woman's behavior changes as she goes on a visit to her natal home. She bids farewell to her husband's relatives respectfully by touching their feet. When she gets into the bus, she keeps her head covered, conducts herself in the usual subdued manner. But as the bus nears her old home, she becomes more relaxed. "As she alights, she seems a different person from the deferential creature she started out, greeting her kin and friends with exuberant embraces." The entire social world of many village women consists of these two contrasting venues, the place where she is the constrained daughter-in-law and the wonderfully freer home in which she is the beloved daughter (Sharma 1980:41, 136).

A Hindu woman veils from no one of her native village. Indeed, it may be considered a breach of etiquette if she should happen to do so, as though she were treating her father as a father-in-law. There she has her confidantes, her girlhood friends who may also be visiting and perhaps also a brother's wife, who are the only ones, other than her mother, with whom she can open her heart and talk about her marriage and sexual experiences. Here, too, she has a more active social life, attending more festival celebrations and women's songfests than she is usually allowed to enjoy in the other village (cf. Jacobson 1970:137, 149, 152; 1982:89–90).

She brings her small children with her. Typically these children long remember the pleasures of these visits. After they are grown men and women they may still feel the glow of visiting their mother's natal village, the special place where she and they were especially cherished. Only when her husband or one of his kinsmen comes to escort her back does she resume her more subdued demeanor. She particularly avoids any exchange with her husband in her natal home because she does not want, in the place where she was unmarried daughter and girl, to make any explicit reminder of her status as wife and sexual partner (Vatuk 1982:74). Hindus of the north generally insist on village exogamy. It is one way of ensuring that a family's affines are kept at a safe distance. Occasionally, and for special reasons, a Hindu girl is married to a man of the same northern village. When that occurs in Nimkhera village, her role as daughter of the village is placed above that as daughter-in-law. She then veils only to her husband and his close kin. She does not veil before the other villagers to whom she remains a village daughter (Jacobson 1970:149; 1982:92).

Muslims do not require village exogamy, but many Muslim brides do come from other villages or towns. They, too, much enjoy visits to their old home (cf. Nath 1981:18; Aziz 1979:28) and are received there as daughters of the village, but whether a Muslim woman goes about that village bare-faced depends partly on her age and status, partly on the will of her husband and family elders.

Another source of personal reward for many women lies in religion. Women are responsible for numerous domestic rites and for women's ceremonies. These ceremonies provide opportunities to take the initiative in community endeavors. Men have various avenues for recreation, for sociability and emotional expression; women find theirs mainly in religion (cf. Luschinsky 1962:718).

As a woman performs the round of daily and monthly domestic rites, as she participates in the annual round of ceremonies, she generally feels that she is protecting and promoting the welfare of her family, her kindred, and all who are dear to her. When these acts require some personal sacrifice, it is pain or loss that she feels will be rewarded, if not sooner, then later. She usually gains quiet satisfaction from the ceremonies in which she must be a passive spectator and finds comfort in those in which she has an active role to play. And when she goes on a pilgrimage, a great adventure for most women, she tours a different and wider landscape from that of her narrow everyday ambit, meets with different people, lives a different life, all under the most propitious of auspices (cf.

*Any woman can manipulate the veil
to convey personal expression.*

Karve 1962; Ali 1917:23–24, 99–100; Minault 1982:253; Jacobson 1977a:94–100).

Though in the traditional mode women are excluded from public affairs, a woman can have influence and power within her domestic sphere, the arena in which she is totally involved and from which she derives so much of her personal satisfactions. A woman's influence in her household normally increases, as we have noted, from very little as a young wife to a great deal as senior matron or dowager. But even a young wife can usually find personal allies in the male camp, among the men before whom she does not veil—her brothers and father, possibly her husband's younger brothers, and her mother's brothers.

She can manipulate the veil itself to convey personal expression behind the impersonal cloth. Pakistani women, Hanna Papanek observes, can express many degrees of modesty or provocation by shifting and redraping their veiling garments. They typically do so to suit any change in the social situation. Papanek makes no mention of Muslim women covering their faces before male kin in their own homes, however (1982[1973]: 11[295–96]). And among the Hindu women whom Ursula Sharma studied, "... it is still possible to flirt or quarrel from behind a veil, and I have seen it done" (1978:226).

A woman may manipulate more than the veiling cloth. Carroll Pastner tells how the women she knew in Panjgur oasis of Pakistani Baluchistan may try to get their own way by such means as much complaining, by pleading illness, playing off male affines and consanguines against each other, and by non-cooperation (1974: 411).* These devices are not unknown in families of other places though their efficacy depends on the particular constellation of family relations, the woman's strength of character, that of other family members, and the woman's ability to work such stratagems discreetly, never blatantly breaching the proprieties of purdah.† Mahatma Gandhi recalled how, in the early years of his marriage, his wife had taught him "the art and practice of non-violent non-cooperation" (Pyarelal 1965:205).

The men of a family may be quite aware of the power potential of the women, at least of their potential for negation. Among the Pirzada of Delhi, Patricia Jeffery reports, the men rely on the women not to sabotage the system of social relations seriously. "The economic power of the men is crucial but its exercise is checked by the possibility of retaliation by the women." One social

---

* "Withdrawal of sexual favors" is listed, but, at least among couples elsewhere in these regions, this is not likely to be flat refusal by a wife, but her assiduous summoning of the many possible reasons and taboos, religious or mundane, for postponing intercourse (cf. Mandelbaum 1974:65, 66).

† Occasionally a strong-willed woman, particularly if well-fortified economically and emotionally, will flout convention, even go everywhere unveiled. Mildred Luschinsky records the case of one such woman in a village near Lucknow (1962:313, 343).

function in which the Pirzada women have strong influence is in the important process of matchmaking. They have their own networks of friendship, visiting, and gossip; they can look over eligible girls in their homes and are better able to assess prospective brides and grooms (1979:171).

So also in the villages studied by Ursula Sharma. Women there can play an important role in matchmaking because they serve as connecting links between their conjugal and natal families in separate villages; within their village they are "informal ambassadors for their households in the community" (Sharma 1980: 150). Negotiations for a marriage are generally of absorbing concern to a family. Its women are usually principals in the discussions, though undercover and behind the public scene. While the legal authority for the bestowal of a girl lies with her father or brother, the mother or grandmother has a very important, sometimes a decisive say about a proposed match (cf. V. Das 1973:37; Vatuk 1972:82).

In sum, though a woman's conduct and movements are much more constrained than are those of a man, women's personalities are not thereby constricted, dispirited, or impassive. Some observers have reported their impressions that, on the whole, the women seem less conflicted and troubled than are the generality of men. To be sure, women who are wrung by poverty, crippled by illness, perhaps afflicted with barrenness, or physically abused by their husbands can scarcely sustain a buoyant personality. But most village women do find gratifying personal rewards, or look forward to such satisfactions in their traditional roles. Urban women who have dropped some purdah practices because of their education or environment, may still want to retain certain aspects of purdah in their own lives. In cities as well as in villages, many women get personal satisfactions from the domestic functions in which they necessarily have greatest interest. Matchmaking, weddings and other domestic occasions provide one source of personal satisfaction; religious devotions and ceremonies provide another. There is visiting and the comfort of gossip. Most sustaining of all are the pleasures and even the vexations from one's children.

CHILDHOOD AND ITS CONSEQUENCES

During their earliest years, village children grow up in the women's quarters and learn the basics of the culture largely from women. When they are able to walk, both boys and girls move quite freely between the men's and the women's spaces and carry messages from one to the other. Girls remain with the women but when a boy learns, at some time after the age of four or five, that he should not stay with the women on pain of derision, he begins to sleep and congregate among the men.

This transition is discussed from a psychoanalytic perspective by Sudhir Kakar (1978) and from a psychological-anthropological perspective by Leigh Minturn. Her account describes child training among the Rajputs of Khalapur village some ninety miles north of Delhi (Minturn and Hitchcock 1966:139–55). As we have noted, Rajputs are the dominant caste, numbering about two thousand in a village population of about five thousand. This account, based on general ethnological observations and intensive interviews with twenty-four mothers, was done as part of a study directed by Beatrice and John Whiting, of child development in six cultures (1965).

Strongly emphasized in the training of these Rajput children are the qualities of obedience, deference, respect—common emphases among people oriented to the prevalence and immanence of hierarchy (Minturn and Hitchcock 1966:120; see also Luschinsky 1962:96; Mandelbaum 1970:120–23; Minturn and Lambert 1964:232). But while all agree that human relations are and should be hierarchical, each person does not necessarily accept the rank assigned to her or him within a particular hierarchy. One indication of this, reported from Khalapur and from elsewhere in India, is the belief that children should not be praised in their hearing lest this make them disobedient. The implications are that a child's deference cannot be taken for granted, that a child who hears such praise will become too self-important to behave in a properly deferential manner. This applies to both girls and boys. It recalls a postulate we have noted before, that social superiority must constantly be reaffirmed and that no one's subordinate position can otherwise be assumed. There seems to be something in this mode of child-rearing that fosters an unbowed spirit as well as a dutifully bowed head (cf. Minturn and Hitchcock 1966:120; Minturn and Lambert 1964:232; Lindholm 1982:171, 197).

The Rajputs of Khalapur show the strong preference for having sons that is typical through all of South Asia. The sons of a family are favored over the daughters in being given better food if food is scarce and better medical attention if many are ill. We shall discuss the demographic and social consequences of these preferences in a later section.

When pregnant women in the Khalapur sample were asked what sex they wanted the child to be, the most frequent reply was a son. But when all the women were asked "whether they *like* boys or girls, mothers say that they like girls, or that they have no preference, and very few report preferring boys." On a scale measuring expressions of maternal warmth, these mothers are less warm and more hostile to boys than to girls. They tend to subject boys more than girls to "frequent physical punishment." Mothers are reluctant to ask their daughters to do household work "because a girl is considered to be a guest in her own home." She will be married off soon after her puberty into another household. There as a daughter-in-law she will be worked hard and perhaps be subjected to harsh authority, so she should be treated hospitably in her natal home (Minturn and Lambert 1964:232–35).

A boy of Khalapur, Beatrice Whiting has suggested, undergoes a conflict not experienced by girls. It arises when he learns that his cozy place with the women is most inferior. "The separation of the sexes leads to a conflict of identity in the boy children, to unconscious fear of being feminine, which leads to 'protest masculinity', exaggeration of the difference between men and women, antagonism against and fear of women, male solidarity, and hence to isolation of women and very young children" (B. Whiting 1965: 137).

This is a tentative hypothesis based on a sample from one vil-

Young boys live among the women of the family
until they are about four or five years old.

lage, but it is congruent with the more ample interpretation of
common childhood experiences in India given by Sudhir Kakar
(1978), a psychoanalyst based in New Delhi. Kakar derives his
analysis from his own clinical observations, from relevant anthropological studies, and from his explications of Hindu myths. While
Muslims do not share the same scriptural and folkloristic themes,
the pivotal experiences of Muslim children are probably much like
those depicted by Kakar for Hindu children.

The most consequential of these modal experiences, according
to both Kakar and Minturn, are the painful disjunctions in their
lives undergone by both boys and girls. These occur at a different
time of life for each sex. They are of a different kind, and have
different aftereffects. A boy must shift, at about age five (for some
a bit earlier, for others later) from the secluded space and separate
world of the women to the company of men. A girl's abrupt change
comes after her puberty, when she moves from the home and vil-

lage where she is daughter into the household and village where she is wife and daughter-in-law.

The cultural devaluation of women, Kakar writes, is not translated by a girl into a sense of worthlessness or low self-esteem. For one reason, in their infancy, "Indian girls are assured of their worth by whom it really matters: by their mothers." A mother's unconscious identification with her daughter is normally stronger than with her son, manifest preferences to the contrary notwithstanding. As an Indian girl grows up in a joint family, "there is almost always someone in particular who gives a little girl the kind of admiration and sense of being singled out as special that a male child more often receives from many." The women of the family are her teachers and models and can also be her allies against any abrasions from the outside (Kakar 1978:60–61).

Up to age four or five, as Kakar draws the normative profile, a child enjoys quick, responsive, and reliable care so that "an Indian generally emerges from infancy into childhood with a staunch belief that the world is benign and that others can be counted on to act in his behalf." Both girls and boys gain that confidence. As a girl approaches puberty and marriage, her training by her mother is "normally leavened with a good deal of compassion" (1978:63, 82).

Then comes the event, deliciously and fearfully anticipated, of her marriage. It is, as we have noted, expected to be a difficult passage and often enough it is so experienced and remembered. But it is a testing for which a girl has been prepared by the general ambience of her culture as well as by direct instruction from her family. With motherhood, she comes into her own as a woman and, especially as the mother of sons, she gains a more secure, prideful place in her family and community. "This accounts for her unique sense of maternal obligation and her readiness for practically unlimited emotional investment in her children" (Kakar 1978:82).

That heavy investment creates an emotional dilemma for a son. The image of the good mother, Kakar finds, is held dear by men of all classes and regions of India. When his male patients begin psychotherapy (a rather rarified sample, to be sure), "patient after patient invariably portrays his mother as highly supportive and extremely loving." Women patients do not recollect their mothers in this adoring way; she is a more earthy figure, "not always benign but always *there*" (1978:82).

Yet a son comes to feel uncomfortable, at an early age, under his mother's lavish attention. "Faced with her unconscious intimations and demands, he may feel confused, helpless and inadequate...." Kakar does not specify the nature of the intimations and demands; more information on these is needed to sustain his formulation. Nor do we have wider information with which to appraise Minturn's observations in Khalapur village that boys are punished more and that girls are liked better by mothers. The misgivings aroused in a son by his mother's fulsome attentions, Kakar suggests, cause many men to harbor an image of a bad mother as well as a good one. Complementing his conscious image of a reliable, loving figure, there is the less conscious suspicion of a capricious, sexually foreboding female. Fantasy about this duality appears in myth and ritual as the mother goddess who is both nurturing benefactress and threatening seductress (Kakar 1978:91–93).

Kakar's exposition here does not square well with anthropological observation that in a traditional joint family, several women share in the care of any one child. A mother, especially a young mother, is so often engaged in household and other work that frequently another woman of the household must look after her infant or toddler. It is rather in urban, educated, nuclear families that a mother is the sole caretaker and the child is the constant focus of her attention (cf. Seymour 1975). Yet in traditional joint families a mother does take over the child in the evening when her chores are done and a child sleeps the night in the embrace of its mother until perhaps the age of four or until a new baby is born. Kakar calls a young village boy's abrupt shift from the indulgent, tender compass of women a second birth for a male at which time he undergoes the shock of entering a different, chillier social atmosphere of the sterner, less sympathetic company of men. There affection and approval are conditional on his good behavior. He is more frequently punished for being troublesome. Without any preparations for the transition, he is banished from the place where he was admired and gently teased to the harsher haunts where he is expected to conform to rules and discharge responsibilities. A popular proverb has it that a son should be treated like a raja, a king, for the first five years, like a slave for the next ten, and like a friend thereafter. Little wonder, Kakar writes, that for a boy this transition "is associated with intense bewilderment, uprootedness and misunderstanding" (1978:127).

In his new surroundings, the youngster typically gets little support from his father. As we have noted, a father is not supposed to show particular interest in his children in the presence of others, lest that create suspicions of favoritism and produce other tensions within the joint family. A man is expected to be equally caring about the sons of his brothers and, if anything, to be more distant from his own sons. If a boy wants something that requires his father's consent, he usually asks one of his father's brothers (or someone in similar kinship relation) to make the request for him. But behind the requisite facade of aloofness and impartiality, the father may well be trying to express his great affection for his own son. As he does, Kakar writes, the boy "is exposed to bewildering contradictory messages of simultaneous love and mistrust, emanating from his father's behaviour" (1978:131–32).

We should note that not all boys grow up in a traditional joint family. Some are in the formative years of their childhood while their family is in the nuclear phase of the cycle of family development (cf. Mandelbaum 1970:95–133). Among poor people, nuclear families are more common since their joint families tend to have only a brief tenure. And urban families now tend to be nuclear, especially among the educated, more affluent classes. Further studies may well show that the effects of joint family living, as drawn by Kakar, occur in nuclear families also, though perhaps with lesser intensity.

Mothers in nuclear families also have their principal interests vested in their children. Fathers in nuclear families as well are supposed to be more aloof than comradely with young sons. Even an urban boy is derided if his schoolmates suspect that he is still fond of being snug in the company of his mother and other women. The number and order of a child's siblings are relevant factors. A boy who is the first born and the only son during his first five years is likely to be given a degree of attention not available to one who is the third of four sons born in quick succession. There are some indications that childhood experiences in educated, urban families still resemble, in important ways, those of the traditional joint family (cf. Vatuk 1972:190–200).

The critical early experiences which Kakar traces are consequences, at least in part, of purdah values and practices. Thus the intensity of a young mother's relation to her children may be the more fervent because of the few other avenues for personal gratification open to a young woman. Separation of living spaces by gender is a basic factor in the shock to a boy when he is shut off from the women's place and must abide in the space and society of the men. That shock, we should note, has so far been inferred rather than observed.

Kakar finds that one result of this experience is a characteristic quality of "narcissistic vulnerability and self-absorption" (1978: 133). That is, the trauma of the early transition leaves a deep impression on a man's self-esteem. He may well feel himself to be a very worthy person, as his first environment encouraged him to believe. But the effects of the second environment plant an equally lasting doubt about his worth that he must constantly try to allay. The effects of a Muslim boy's circumcision at about age eight on the formation of his personality have not, to my knowledge, yet been studied.

Another inferred consequence is the "passive-receptive attitude toward authority figures of all kinds" (ibid., 1978:134). That is, a man never loses his identification with his bountiful mother and transposes her demure conduct before elders to his own adult relations toward respected others. A man's inclination toward hierarchical social frames is rooted, Kakar believes, in the apprenticelike relation to males that he had to adopt when he was plunged among the men.

We can note that it is in the company of the men that a boy learns the rules of his jati, his caste group. He discovers the modes of competition and cooperation, he finds out who are the enemies of his kin and what needs to be defended. He has picked up the basics of the culture and the language among the women; among the men he absorbs the basics of the male social order, the rules of engagement, of alliance and manipulation, and the purposes for social striving, of izzat.

Kakar says that Indian children learn to comply with the standards of the group in which they are participating at any given time more than with the norms that they may previously have absorbed. In a boy, this may be related to his taking on the roles and rules of the men's arena after absorbing the different ways of the women's quarters. The internal sentinels of the superego are not by any means absent, but are likely to be adapted to a current situation and to the standards of one's immediate group.

Hence, Kakar writes, people in India tend to show greater reliance on external authority and less on internal promptings. A man feels the need of an authority figure he can idealize and has a "reflexive reverence for superiors." In religion, a good many Hindu men and women seek out a *guru*, a mentor of purity and authority who can be idealized. In an influential book, widely read among South Asian Muslims since its first publication in 1905, each Muslim man and woman is urged to find and commit himself/herself to such a master and teacher (Metcalf 1984:188). In politics, a man who presents himself as a strong, dedicated leader and has some success, is likely to attract followers who are also devotees (ibid., 137–38). But should a person's confidence in the reigning authority be shaken, should he come to doubt the legitimacy and worthiness of the hitherto superior group or leader, then he is likely to reject them violently.

His fury is then directed against the very people to whom he formerly gave reverence. Kakar notes that the intensity of the male's transition shock and the resulting buildup of anger is greatest where purdah is most strictly observed. "In communities that emphasize manliness in its *machismo* elaboration and keep their women in the seclusion of purdah—for example, the Rajputs—and who thus exact from their sons a dramatic and total renunciation of the feminine world of mothers and sisters and aunts, the 'oedipal' dimension of boyish rage against the father and other males tends to be more pronounced than in communities where the second birth is a more relaxed or gradual process" (ibid., 134).

This sketch of Kakar's argument cannot do justice to the scope and depth of his presentation. Like the best of the Freudian writings, beginning with those of the eponymous ancestor himself, the work opens new vistas for further investigation. While we need much more firm evidence on the behavior which Kakar discusses, more rigorous demonstration of causes and effects, more attention to regional and other variations, his book does provide insights on interaction between purdah practices and personality configurations. The separation of the women's domain from that of the men and the constraints on women's activities clearly do affect personality formation in children. They, in turn, grow up to be men and women who want to carry on with purdah practices and values. There is indeed reciprocal influence, a "mutual reinforcement of psyche and culture" (ibid., 182).

CHAPTER 4

Effects and Meanings
of Purdah-Izzat

The effects of purdah reach into
much of social life, including economic, matrimonial, educational,
and political concerns. One economic consequence of having
women keep within the household is that women's labor, especially in the fields, is curtailed. But that does not necessarily diminish productivity greatly. In some communities, even women
in purdah may do some outside work. Caste groups like the Jats,
who are dominant in many villages of western U. P. and Haryana,
generally prize diligent work and good harvests above the stricter
requirements of purdah.

Moreover, most village women, whatever their degree of purdah practice, work hard at tasks inside the household, in cooking,
cleaning, preparing milk and food products, caring for animals, and
assisting with family manufactures. Where modern technology has
replaced some kinds of women's work, as the power mill and fod-
der cutter have, most women still work through an endless day.
Nor have modern agricultural developments altered, at least not
yet, women's economic position. In the villages studied by Ursula
Sharma, the advent of a cash economy and capitalist production
have not lessened the economic dependence of women on men. "If
anything it increases it by adding to their old dependence on men
as property holders a new dependence on men as wage earners"
(1980:132, 207). And the system of purdah is partly based on the

economic dependence of women, particularly on their exclusion from control over productive resources (cf. Sanday 1973).

That dependence, Barbara Miller points out for rural India, is less in those regions where women make important contributions to the cultivation of staple crops. Women provide much labor in the growing of rice; they provide relatively little in the growing of wheat. The wheat-growing lands of the subcontinent are also most of those in which purdah practices are strong. In the Dravidian-speaking south, the staple is rice, raised by labor-intensive transplantation, and, as we have noted, restrictions on women there are much less stringent and central (Miller 1981:107–32).

Miller remarks and summarizes much data from census reports and ethnographic sources and finds that women's labor and earnings are more important to families of the "unpropertied" classes throughout India. Among the poorer groups there are less rigorous constraints on women than there are among the propertied groups, especially in the north (1981:27, 74–80). "Work makes worth" is the phrase with which Miller summarizes her hypothesis (1981: 110–32). It should be tested by such means as studying gender relations where the less labor-intensive, broadcast method of raising paddy is used and by further comparisons in the rice-growing parts of West Bengal and Bangladesh.

Another study measures the importance of women's labor in wet-paddy cultivation. Pranab Bardhan cites a 1971 survey, done by M. R. Rosenzweig and T. P. Schultz, of 1,334 rural households in India. The first stage of the analysis shows that there is a significant positive correlation between district-level normal rainfall and the probability that a woman is employed in rural India. The second stage "confirms that the differential survival chance of the female child improves with higher female employment rates or with a lower male-female earning differential per day" (Bardhan 1982:1450). That is, more girl children survive in rural India where women's work is important to the family income and to the agricultural economy; more die where it is not.

These stark demographic facts are indicated in the title of Barbara Miller's book, *The Endangered Sex* (1981). Her study shows that female infanticide occurred principally among the higher jatis in the northern regions of India before the British government banned the practice (Miller 1981:49–67). And census statistics show that there have been more males than females in the states of northwest India than is true elsewhere in India (Miller 1981:71). In the 1981 Census of India, the ratio of females per thousand males (as given in Provisional Population Table 7) was 886 in Punjab, 877 in Haryana, and 886 in Uttar Pradesh. The sex ratios in other northern states was more like those in the four southern states, Kerala 1,034, Tamil Nadu 978, Andhra Pradesh 975, and Karnataka 963. This disparity is region-specific rather than religion-specific. Bardhan points out that in the 1971 census, the sex ratio for Muslims in Uttar Pradesh was about the same as for the whole population of that state while the ratio for Muslims in Kerala was much different, with more females than males, similar to the ratio of Kerala state as a whole (Bardhan 1982:1148).

The preponderance of males in the northern and northwestern states of India results mainly from the greater mortality rate for juvenile girls, from infancy to age 10, than for boys in the same age range (Miller 1981:80–82, 156–59). The causes of these greater survival rates for boys, Miller finds, are that boys are given better and longer medical care than are girls; they get better nutrition; they are given more "love and warmth." Miller cites the evidence of hospital admissions to show that boys are given better medical care. Ethnographic descriptions indicate that they also get the better food of whatever is available to a family (1981:83–102).

Given the marked preference for sons, it would seem likely that sons receive more and stronger expressions of love than do daughters (Miller 1981:102–06). But the case is not clear. The one study which attempted to measure maternal expressions of warmth was done with a small sample of Rajput mothers of Khalapur village. It shows that these mothers were less warm and more hostile to sons than to daughters. Yet when pregnant women of the village were asked about their preference, they said that they preferred bearing a son rather than a daughter (Minturn and Lambert 1964:232–35).

Preference for sons, rather than deliberate neglect of daughters, seems to be the primary reason for discrimination in medical care and food. Miller discusses several reasons for son preference, including benefits at inheritance, ritual requirements, support for parents in their old age, and the heavy costs of marrying a daughter (1981:137–59). These account for the less joyous reception of a female newborn than of a male, especially when the parents have no sons, or have more daughters than sons. But there is little evidence that a daughter typically feels rejected in her family and, especially in the years just before her marriage, a daughter is likely to get special, loving care.

In the twentieth century, dowry payments and other costs of marrying off a daughter honorably have risen sharply and the custom of giving dowries has been adopted among many groups who formerly did not do so. The transfer of valuables, including money, by the bride's family to the groom's family is an ancient practice among Hindus. Muslim tradition required only that a bride bring a trousseau, an array of things to be worn and used by herself and the family in her new home. Money and other valuables were not usually transferred in a traditional Muslim marriage. In recent decades, however, the parents of an esteemed Muslim young man have been demanding and getting large dowry payments (cf. S. A. Husain 1976:119–37; Aziz 1979:66–68; Jeffery 1979:32–33, 134–35).

Bride-price or bride-wealth, the reverse of dowry, is given at marriage in some groups, mainly those of lower caste rank or of tribal organization, and more often in the South than in the North (cf. Miller 1981:146–48).

A marriage usually involves multiple transactions, and both families give something on the occasion of a new union. In dowry systems, the bride givers expend far more than do the bride receivers. Randaria and Visaria cite marriage practices among the lower-ranking castes of North Gujerat, among whom the bride receivers traditionally pay a fixed amount to the family of the bride, but they receive much more from her family (1984:649). In many of the groups in which the groom's family presents a substantial payment to the family of the bride, women's labor contributes importantly to the subsistence economy and such payments can be understood as a partial or a token compensation to the bride's family for the loss of her services.

Some of the groups in which bride-wealth was customarily paid, have now switched to giving dowries instead. The reasons seem to have more to do with the contribution of a marriage to family status than with the contribution of the women to family economy. People who paid bride-wealth have long known that the giving of dowry was the custom of the higher-ranking groups and so was the more prestigious practice. With changing economic and political tides, many of them now are able to compete for better ranking, within their jati as well as among jatis, in ways they formerly could not emulate. Taking on the custom of dowry payment is, like the adoption of stricter purdah, one of the traditional hallmarks of superior status (cf. Towards Equality 1974: 69–70; Sharma 1980:137–40; Miller 1981:139–54; Rajaram 1983; Kolenda 1984:108).*

The amount of a dowry in families of middle or high rank may come to a year's income or more for the bride's family. Those families whose members cannot amass such sums, even those on whom hunger presses from time to time, still try to scrape up the

* An analysis of the reasons for the shift from bride-price to dowry payments in villages of Mandya District of Karnataka (formerly Mysore) applies also to similar changes in northern villages. Scarlett Epstein gives four causes for this change among the "Peasant" caste of these villages. First is the increased wealth which these cultivators now have. They can spend more lavishly on weddings and on other means of raising their social standing in the community. It is now a matter of prestige to remove women from working in the fields. Young girls, no longer required to do field labor, require more costly jewelry. "Where formerly a Peasant's wife was an economic asset, she has now become a liability. Accordingly, the groom's family now want to be paid for taking over the responsibility for keeping her, where previously they had been prepared to compensate her father for the loss of her productive contribution." Further, there is now a small but growing number of young educated men of this caste whose parents claim compensation for their son's education from his bride's family. Lastly, the prestigious Brahmans of this region have the dowry system which the newly affluent Peasants can now adopt (Epstein 1960:199).

equivalent of several months' income to marry off a daughter honorably.

Some students of the subject have suggested that a dowry is a payment of a daughter's share of the family inheritance, given before the parent's death (cf. Goody 1973:17). That explanation does not hold in South Asia. A dowry is not thought of in those terms. A woman has no control over the dowry wealth, nor does she have any priority of claim to it. The payments are to the husband and his family. A more cogent explanation is that the dowry is a partial payment for her future maintenance and an inducement to treat her well (cf. Sharma 1980:142–43). The latter consideration is usually much on the minds of her close kin during the marriage negotiations. She is going into a new, uncertain, possibly hostile household.

If they give skimpily, her lot there will not be improved and will probably be worsened. If they give lavishly, not only will their beloved daughter's chances for a happier home be increased, but their own prestige will be heightened. The prestige of the groom's family will also be enhanced by a bounteous dowry, a measure of the worth of their son and his kin. Nor is the dowry a final payment. A woman's natal family is usually obliged, for the sake of her well-being and of their honor, to keep giving gifts to her and to her marital family on the proper occasions, particularly in the early years of her marriage (Towards Equality 1974:71).

Most families, whether of high or of low rank, aspire to elevate, or at least sustain, their status and reputation. A rise in public esteem is, as we have noted, best validated and ratified through the marriage of daughters into families of suitable eminence. Hence, a costly wedding and large dowry become necessary investments for family members who seek, as many do in these competitive societies, to enhance their own and their family's izzat.

Another kind of social investment is in education. As we noted earlier, the highroad to upward mobility and sustained high status in the twentieth century has been through education. An educated young man usually has far better prospects for income, security, and prestige than has a man with little or no education. Education is requisite for coveted positions in government service and for the best jobs in commerce and industry. Even for a family of cultivators, it is a great asset to have a son whose education enables him to deal effectively with officialdom.

So a prospective groom with good educational credentials has, other things being equal, great attraction as a marriage partner for one's daughter. But getting such a spouse requires heavy outlays. His family asks for a large dowry, justified as partial recompense for the expenses of educating him. And as we have noted, securing an educated son-in-law also requires commensurate education for one's daughter.

There has been a steady inflation of dowry amounts. One token of cost escalation is in the kind of conveyance provided by the bride's family for the bridegroom when he comes to the bride's home for the wedding. Among the poorer classes, a bridegroom usually comes on a pony, hired for the occasion. More affluent families in town and country put the bridegroom astride a finely-decked white horse, also rented. In the 1950s I first saw a wedding procession in Bombay in which the bridegroom was riding in an open white Cadillac. That has been topped in recent years by at least one bridegroom's family that demanded and got a helicopter to bring them to the wedding (Towards Equality 1974:74).

An escalation in dowry payments that arouses particular bitterness stems from family wealth that has been amassed from the black market and other illegal sources. "A new class of nouveau riche has emerged that buys a daughter's fortune with dowry, to raise its own social status by entering into marriage alliances with families of high status." Extravagant spending on weddings is one way of disposing of black market money with little chance of being questioned. "Men of honest means and moderate income find it extremely difficult to remain honest in order to compete with this class that has a free flow of black money" (Towards Equality 1974:76).

Complaints about the cruel hardships this inflation imposed on families with more daughters than sons led to the passage of a law in India prohibiting dowries. But the distinguished Committee on the Status of Women in India reported in 1974, "We are compelled to record our finding that the Dowry Prohibition Act of 1961, passed with the ostensible purpose of curbing this evil, if not eradicating it, has signally failed to achieve its purpose" (Towards Equality 1974:115). The strong drive to maintain and enhance family honor through a daughter's marriage has not been perceptibly diminished by the passage of a federal law. Amassing a prestigious patrimony for one's sons still requires assiduous success in the matrimony of one's daughters.

The defects of the Dowry Act were so glaring that, after pressure from women's organizations and after a report on the dowry issue from a Joint Committee of the Indian Parliament, the Dowry Prohibition (Amended) Bill was passed in 1984. But the amended bill is little stronger than the 1961 law and gives small promise of being more effective in curbing the practice of large dowry payments ("S. V." 1984:1609–10).

The restrictions of purdah also constrain the education of girls. At every educational level, the proportion of girls in school is far lower than that of boys. In India about two-thirds of the girls aged 6 through 11 are enrolled in a school; actual attendance is much less, the drop-out rate is very high. About one in seven of the girls aged 14 through 17 is enrolled in a secondary school (Towards Equality 1974:234–82). The statistics for girls' education in Pakistan and Bangladesh show similar disparities.

Poor families usually do not keep their daughters in school for long or send them there at all because they cannot afford the small expense of doing so and because they do not want to forego the benefits of their work at household chores and baby-tending. In families not quite so poverty-stricken, a daughter may be allowed to attend the primary grades but is taken out of school as she approaches puberty. If a village girl must travel more than a short distance to school, the possible perils of that trip may bar her further attendance (cf. Jacobson 1977b:220–23).

Girls' classes are usually separate from those of boys, except for the first primary grades. They are typically taught by women teachers and this gives employment to women with appropriate education. Women teachers have to cope with the personal problems posed by purdah standards. Some of them meet resistance from their families, "partly from the general apprehension about women working away from home and partly from a fear of personal insecurity in villages" (Towards Equality 1974:260). Against these limitations there are countervailing pressures to educate a daughter, set by families who can afford the costs, in order to secure a suitably worthy, educated husband for her.

One of Gandhi's more radical acts was his call for women to participate actively in the struggle for independence, a call, as we have seen from Nehru's comment, to which a good many women responded. It was squarely counter to the purdah taboo on women taking any part in public political affairs. After independence, all women gained the right to vote in all governmental elections; women have been elected to high political office since then, both in the central and state governments. The incidence in India of women elected to Parliament has been about the same as it is in the U. S. House of Representatives. In villages and town neighborhoods there is commonly some, but not much, participation by women in local politics (cf. Jacobson 1977b:236–39). As we have noted, educated women who participate in higher-level politics are judged by different, more tolerant standards than are the great preponderance of wives and daughters. But both standards answer to the same question of how much honor or dishonor befalls her family by a woman's conduct.

The advent of electoral politics has brought, in addition to democratic advantages, a new dimension to the oppositions among village factions. Very rarely does a woman take part in any public airing of factional disputes. But many a matron lets husband and son know, especially when she is serving their meals and they are pinned in place, what they must do in a local dispute if they are to act like true men. And what they do when they act like true men is influenced, at many turns, by their values about izzat and purdah.

SYMBOLS, MEANINGS, AND VALUES

As symbolic behavior, purdah practices communicate strong, pervasive, primordial meanings. They are strong in that palpable failure to produce them by the proper gestures in the proper situations may arouse strong emotional reaction. They are pervasive in that these acts and meanings are not limited to any single part of a culture or to a particular social group; the underlying values infuse many aspects of culture and society in these regions. They are primordial in two senses. They help provide answers to a basic question, that of relations between male and female, to which every society develops some reply. The response at any one time is but the most recent of a long series. These responses are also primordial in the individual's experience, imprinted on a person from early childhood. They are deeply, emotionally rooted in each individual, in her and his personality and life-history. So the meanings conveyed by purdah observances are both phylogenetically and ontogenetically primordial.

What then, are these meanings about? We have distinguished two general meanings. The more explicit and conscious one is about the dangers to women outside their own households from male strangers. The other, usually couched in terms of "showing respect" is about the dangers from women, as son's wives, to harmony and order inside the household. Both carry further, implicit meanings. The idea of women imperiled outside rests on ideas about the innate nature of women and of men. Women are expected to view male strangers as possibly predatory, presumptively untrustworthy, and potentially aggressive. Against them, her close male kin are her protectors. Some males need not be feared because of considerations of age, friendship, kinship, or special, often religious, allegiance.

A related postulate about gender is expressed in the common metaphor about human reproduction. The man is said to provide the seed, the woman the field. The man's part is active and determinative, the woman's passive and nurturing. Moreover, some say, because the seed determines the nature of the child, men must protect and control women to be sure that the children born to a woman are of her husband's seed. And, as in most though not all societies, it is believed to be in the nature of man to be extremely touchy on this point of honor, to want to be both genitor and pater, biological as well as social father to the children born of his wife (cf. Beech 1982:113; Yalman 1963).

Women, in the view of the men of these regions, are passive and subordinate before male challenge, though some women may possess dark powers and can manage to be wayward. As we have noted, Hindu scripture and folklore elaborate the dual nature of women in the character of goddesses who are nurturing and benevolent yet can also be destructive and malevolent (cf. Babb 1975; O'Flaherty 1980; Wadley 1977).

One belief about the danger to men from women is that sexual intercourse weakens a man because of the loss of life-sustaining semen. Another danger from woman rises from her reproductive functions. During menstruation and after child-birth, a woman, whether Hindu or Muslim, observes more rigorous seclusion than usual. At these periods she poses special dangers to others and is herself in a ritually vulnerable state. Hindus hold that bodily emissions are ritually polluting; the emissions of menstruation and childbirth are more parlous than any others.

Girl children, as Paul Hershman observed in a village of central Punjab, are taught from an early age that the vagina is a source of shame and impurity which must always be kept concealed. Boys go about without clothes until they are four or five; a mother may then tease her son about his nakedness. As a virgin, a girl is ritually pure enough to be worshipfully treated on certain ceremonial occasions. "Virginity and motherhood are both highly esteemed states in Punjabi society but wifehood and sexuality are those aspects which devalue a woman and render her the inferior of a man" (1977:272, 275).

Hershman discusses the seeming contradiction between the high value placed on motherhood and female fertility on the one side, and the gross ritual impurity of female sexuality and of childbirth on the other. His analysis suggests that the contradiction is "resolved" for Hindus primarily through two ritual symbols, the goddess who is both virgin and mother, and the cow which, though animal, figures as the untainted motherly aspect of womanhood. But he also concludes that this and other apparent contradictions exist in the eyes and mind of the anthropologist rather than in those of the people; "the Punjabis conceive of the goddess in some contexts as a virgin and in others as a mother, but they never bring the two together to form a contradiction of which they themselves would be aware" (ibid., 290–91).

So the unceasing veilings and distancings within a household imply a societal meaning. They bespeak, as we have noted, a need to keep women as wives in their subordinate place, one in which they have less chance to disrupt the vital yet delicate bonds among the men. Further, in-house purdah observances reaffirm the social order of the family which is felt to be as much in need of constant reaffirmation as is the hierarchy of the social world outside.

An incident told by Charlotte Wiser gives a sidelight on this. One day she was sitting with some women of the village in Mainpuri district of Uttar Pradesh where she lived for many years. A young man appeared, shouting a torrent of abuse directed at someone in the group. Then she noticed that the girl at her side was smiling under her veiling scarf. She was his newly married wife whom he was ordering about. She hurried to do his bidding and returned, all smiles. He had demonstrated that he was a proper husband, she had shown that she was a proper wife. Both were satisfied with the public display of their new relationship (Wiser and Wiser 1963:79–81).

Several other meanings are conveyed through purdah practices. A family's economic position and social status, as noted above, are commonly signalled by the degree of purdah observed by its women. On another level, veiling defines the relationship between a woman and a man or between new wife and mother-in-law, and so defines appropriate and inappropriate conduct. Sometimes seemingly contradictory messages are projected. In the Punjab, Paul Hershman noted, a woman may breast-feed her infant in the presence of any man, the nurturing act of motherhood taking precedence over the otherwise rigid taboo against a woman showing her breasts. And while the mother nurses her child, she will also veil herself at the approach of a senior man (1977:274).

However contradictory the juxtaposition of bared breast and veiled face may seem to an outside observer, neither the young mother nor the senior man perceives any contradiction. The veil and the breast-feeding belong to different compartments of behavior, the one to mother-child relations of mutual nurturance, the other to woman-senior man relations of mutual avoidance. Both are key symbols, both stem from deeply held values, and both express major meanings.

CHAPTER 5

Two Versions of Purdah

MUSLIM AND HINDU

So far we have examined the patterns of purdah that are, by and large, common to Muslims and Hindus, indeed to most of the larger ethnic and religious communities of these northern regions. But we have also noted a number of ways in which Muslim values and conduct differ markedly from those of Hindus. Before appraising such differences we consider the general cultural and social relations between Muslims and Hindus.

Muslims have long been numerically predominant in the westernmost and easternmost sectors of the purdah zone. When, after 1947, these areas became the Islamic states of Pakistan and, later, Bangladesh, there was a considerable movement of non-Muslims out of them, and of Muslims from India into them. Muslims are now about 97 percent of the Pakistani population of 83.8 million (1981), and about 90 percent of Bangladesh's 87 million (1981). In India Muslims were about 11 percent of the total Indian population of 684 million in 1981. In Uttar Pradesh their proportion was about 16 percent of the total state population, 111 million in 1981.

Muslims and Hindus have lived side by side for centuries through most of the purdah zone. Since the great majority of Muslims on the subcontinent are descended from converts to Islam, there are many cultural affinities in each region between the two groupings whose formal religions are so disparate.

A useful source for comparisons of Hindu and Muslim patterns is provided by the volumes on Indian Muslims edited by Imtiaz Ahmad (1976a, 1978a, 1981a). In his overview of the volume on family, Ahmad writes that "Muslim family norms in India correspond closely to those held among Hindus" (1976b:xxii). In his introduction to the volume on caste and stratification he notes that the contributors (with one exception) ". . . are of the view that social stratification among the Muslim communities studied by them is certainly comparable to the Hindu caste system though an exact parallel cannot be said to exist" (1978b:4). In the volume on ritual and religion he concludes, "It is clear that as a practiced faith Islam is far more pluralistic in character than the extreme degree of reification attributed to it by Islamicists and Muslim theologians would admit" (1981b:18). That is, the actual religious beliefs and acts of Indian Muslims include a good deal that is of the country as well as much that is of the Koran and its commentaries.

Ahmad emphasizes the importance of the Koran and of the distinctive Islamic plan for the day, the year, the life. But he also notes that Muslims of the subcontinent "participate simultaneously in both a local and an Islamic culture" (1981b:3). The local components are considerable and vary considerably from region to region (1976b:xx, xxiv). The ways in which Muslims of one region differ from Muslims of another region, as in subsistence patterns and daily life, usually correspond to the ways in which the Hindus of the same regions differ from each other.

Similar though the Muslims and Hindus of a locality may be culturally, in many respects they remain separate socially. There is typically little interchange between them in domestic matters; there are few of the solidary bonds that connect kinsmen. Religious observances are carried on separately, in different ways, at different places. Each side attributes the social separation to their differences in religious ideology.

Yet cooperative engagement is also maintained. Muslims and Hindus within a locality commonly exchange goods and services; there may be some mutual participation in village ceremonies; and all in a village or town neighborhood generally unite against outside encroachment, whether by government officials, natural calamities, or intrusive exploiters. And in India there is now a record of the decades since independence of mutual participation by Muslims, Hindus and other religious-ethnic groups in common national pursuits—administrative, political, commercial, industrial, and educational.

The extent of local social separation has varied from time to time and from region to region (cf. Ahmad 1981b:3–4). From his studies of Kashmir villagers, T. N. Madan concluded that Kashmiri society consists of dual social orders that are accommodated within an overarching framework of common language, customs, and state government. In villagers' perceptions, the duality is far more important than the common frame (Madan 1981:59–61). By contrast, L. M. Bookman's account (1979) of communal relations in a village of Saharanpur district in Uttar Pradesh tells of much cooperation in economic and political affairs as well as of the sharing of some basic values.

When violence broke out in the district during the partition riots of 1947, the Hindu elders called the village Muslims back from the place to which they had fled and successfully protected them when they returned to their homes. In such matters, the Muslims and Hindus of the village act "as members of a common society and culture." But, Bookman adds, in those social situations that touch on the nature of self and society, there is divergence. Muslims identify themselves as Muslims and with Muslims, Hindus with Hindus. There are, to be sure, social cleavages among the village Hindus of different factions and castes, and marked social separations among the four Muslim groups of the village. But on the whole these villagers, as do most others in the land, tend to see Hindus and Muslims as more radically distinct than they appear to be on an inventory of culture traits. Each person considers himself, if it comes to a test, as being either Hindu or Muslim.

It was this perception of difference that underlay the partition of Pakistan from India at the moment of independence. In a paper I wrote at the time (1947), I discussed how the communal outlook had been intensified among the educated middle classes and how it came to prevail as a result of the uncertainties and tensions during World War II and immediately after the war. Partition, like other great political events, grew out of a substratum of everyday perceptions and interactions of which the practice of purdah and its underlying principles form an important element.

The everyday practice of purdah in a Muslim household follows the general pattern we have sketched, but with some notable differences in emphasis and scope (first noted by Jacobson 1970: 6, 13–20, 126–99). A Muslim bride also comes to live with her husband's family. There she may cover her head and face before her husband's father and elder brothers, and avoid direct gaze at or speech with them. But she less often comes as the complete stranger that a Hindu bride of the north usually is. Muslims have a general preference for arranging marriages between two who are already related, as the son and daughter of two brothers, real or classificatory, or as the children of friendly families. A girl who becomes engaged to be married to a kinsman must then veil before the young man, who up to then she has known as a familiar relative (cf. Jeffery 1979:196). Perhaps it is because some Muslim brides come into familiar families that young Muslim wives usually do not have to keep quite as rigorous avoidance within the household as is required of comparable Hindu wives.

Because some of a person's relatives through marriage may also be related through descent, there is not the sharp demarcation between affinal and consanguinal kin that prevails among northern Hindus. Thus a Hindu matron in a Madhya Pradesh village must veil before her children's senior affines, as, for example, to her daughter's mother-in-law, and that woman must veil before her. Muslim women need not keep themselves so meticulously distanced from their affines or their children's (cf. Jacobson 1970: 137, 145, 166–67).

Veiling by Muslim women emphasizes a different dichotomy. It is between those kin and close friends who come within the trusted circle of the family and all others who are considered outsiders. Some of these outsiders may be well known to the family as neighbors or as remoter kin, but they do not come into the inner parts of the home.

Doranne Jacobson's account is particularly illuminating on this score. She tells that among the Pathan Muslims she studied, "the element of trust is central" to purdah observance. Should a woman come to mistrust a close kinsman, she may begin to seclude herself from him. Kinsmen who quarrel may order their wives to veil before their opponents and to avoid the now distanced relatives (1976a:190–91).

Muslim women tend to keep even more strictly to their own quarters of the house, the *zenana*, than do their Hindu counterparts. Larger houses usually have a room at the front entrance beyond which strangers may not go unless invited. Adjoining it is a room in which the men of the family entertain visitors. The women do not enter these outer rooms. Behind them is the courtyard where the family women stay; there they may meet female visitors and trusted men. In the rear of the house is the space where women and small children pass much of the day and where they sleep at night. Even the family men do not usually linger there (cf. Roy 1979:29–30). Where the houses are built with flat-topped roofs and adjoin each other, women visit across the rooftops. They entertain women guests there unless the men want to come up, perhaps to enjoy the cool of the evening. Warned, the women then go back to their courtyard and inner domain.

Within the household, a Muslim woman covers her head or veils her face not only before her husband's father and elder brothers, but also does so before any man among the family intimates who is *namaharam*, "not forbidden" to her, that is, not forbidden as a possible husband. They are the men whom she could have married and who, should she become a widow or divorcee, might be eligible spouses. An educated Muslim woman from Lucknow told Reshma Yunus (1983): "My mother to this day speaks to non-maharam men from behind a partition." A woman does not similarly avoid those men who come into the household and who are not possible husbands, such as her father, brother and sons (cf. Roy 1979:41; Zaidi 1970:54, 153).

Just who among kinsmen and friends should be included within a Muslim family's circle of trust is a matter of choice by the family elders. A Hindu woman's father and brother rarely if ever enter her married home, but such affines may be family intimates in a Muslim household. Thus, on Panjgur oasis in westernmost Pakistan, decisions as to which among related men are allowed to come into the home are "left up to individual households." In villages of Comilla district in Bangladesh, "each family has made its own list, of family insiders" (Pastner 1982:170–71; Zaidi 1970:54).*

Muslim women do not veil before certain classes of men whose roles or life-styles exempt them from the prima facie distrust of strangers. When a woman consults a religious specialist or a holy man about her personal problems, she sits before him with head covered but with face unveiled (cf. Jeffery 1979:40). Veiling before male servants varies by region and class. Pukhtun women in Swat do not keep purdah before house servants or house slaves because such a man "was often considered a sort of junior family member" (Lindholm 1982:105). Perhaps also among these fierce people, a servant whose eyes were too closely fastened on a young woman of the family might soon feel a terrible swift dagger across his throat. In Panjgur also, women do not veil before house servants and men of the lowest rank, sweepers and water-carriers, who are defined as not posing any peril to family (Pastner 1974:110).

Some shopping may be done by older Muslim women. If the family is wealthy enough, merchants bring their wares to the house for examination. More commonly, women may visit shops for

---

* From two Muslim villages of the same Bangladesh district, Bertocci reports an unusually broad definition of family insiders (1974:116). Fellow villagers address one another by kinship terms, the common practice in Bangladesh as in other sections of the northern zone. Quite uncommon among Muslims is the freedom allowed in these villages to a man unrelated to the family to come into a house and speak with the women even in the absence of their men. At the other extreme there are such ultra-rigorous families, as the one reported from Jessore in Bangladesh. Not only was the wife strictly secluded from all but a very few men, but she even had to veil before her husband's younger brother, a relationship that is usually relatively free and familiar (Husain 1956:v. 2, 325).

special purchases, as for a daughter's trousseau. They discuss the goods and prices with the shopkeepers. If he is a long-time purveyor to the family, they may engage in conversation with him.

In general, Muslim women must be vigilant about observing purdah for reasons that are similar to those given by Hindus but with different emphases. Hindu elders are more concerned with the danger to family unity and honor from within, from the younger wives who come as aliens to the family and who may alienate their husbands from it. Muslim family elders are not insensible of such dangers, but are much less perturbed by them. Their affines are, often enough, also consanguines: a new bride is not necessarily perceived as a potential disrupter.* Muslim concerns are much more fixed on the danger to family honor from without, from the encircling world of mistrustable strangers. If a Muslim woman can be more relaxed than her Hindu neighbor about avoidances within the household, she must be more strictly careful about maintaining social invisibility outside (Jacobson 1970:187).

Almost all Muslim men, Zaidi says of Bangladeshis, strongly prefer that the women of their families keep strict purdah "against strangers and distant relatives" (1970:54). The preposition indicates the sentiment; a woman should be perpetually defensive *against* all those outside the family circle of trust. A Muslim woman from Abbotabad in northwest Pakistan told Reshma Yunus (1983) that if a woman is forced by necessity to speak to a man who is a stranger, she should speak to him as if they were enemies. She should use a harsh voice and even be rude, "because if you speak nicely, then he would be attracted to you and this could lead to evil" (personal communication, 1983).

In the Muslim view, girls are invested with this electric attraction when they reach puberty. At that time of their lives they take on the full panoply of purdah (Zaidi 1970:50; Vreede-de Stuers

* Alberuni, whose chronicle of India of the eleventh century is the first Muslim account of Hindu civilization, remarks on this, "According to their marriage laws it is better to marry a stranger than a relative. The more distant the relationship of a woman with regard to her husband the better" (Alberuni 1971: 155). From a Muslim point of view, this was, and is, a curious custom.

1968:78; Jacobson 1970:167). In some families, a girl's puberty is anticipated and she begins her social seclusion between ages nine and twelve. And Shibani Roy notes that among the Muslim families she studied in Delhi and Lucknow, girls in the age range of five to nine are discouraged from playing with boys and from visiting in neighboring households (Roy 1979:70; see also Aziz 1979:56; Abdulla and Zeidenstein 1980:63). In Hindu families, however, a girl does not have to assume purdah observance until she is married. It is her acquisition of a husband and in-laws rather than her sexual maturation that impels her into purdah (cf. Jacobson 1970: 137; Sharma 1978:222).

Sexual attraction is differently phrased, Hanna Papanek notes, by Hindus than it is by the Pakistani Muslim men she has interviewed. Papanek has the impression that Hindu men and family elders tend to see a young woman as the temptress, while Muslims tend rather to believe that both men and women have strong sexual desires which they can control only with difficulty (1982 [1973]: 36 [316–17]). Zarina Bhatty similarly remarks that Indian Muslim men deem strict seclusion to be necessary because a woman "inevitably arouses, by mere appearance, sensual desires in men over which they are not expected to have any self-control" (1976:104).

In all, a Muslim woman of "respectable" family should venture out very little, and then only in the portable seclusion of a *burka*, an all-enveloping garment, and be accompanied, preferably, by a trustworthy companion. When she travels by vehicle, her passenger space should be completely curtained from prying eyes whether the vehicle be an ox-cart, a horse-drawn two-wheeler, a railway compartment, or a Mercedes-Benz. A Hindu woman of similar status usually takes care to cover her head and possibly veil her face when she is within view of strangers, especially when traveling. But Hindu families do not usually insist on the sight-proof outer foil required en route for many Muslim women. Curtains are not usually practical on a bus or airplane; a Muslim woman bus rider has to make do with the shield of her burka and her aloof demeanor. And occasionally, on a city street, one may see a figure in a burka on a scooter, riding side-saddle behind the driver.

*It is not unusual to see a woman dressed in a burka
riding behind her husband on a motorcycle.*

Among a few Hindu groups, as those who were close to the former courts of Rajput rulers, the zeal for stringent observance of
purdah resembled that of Muslims of similar rank. Rama Mehta
has described the high degree of seclusion observed by the women
of the Oswals, a jati that traditionally provided administrators for
the Maharana of Udaipur and other princes of Rajasthan. An Oswal
woman veiled even to the maidservants of her household. When
she went outdoors, she wore a thick sari over her indoor dress. As
the powers of the princes and their courts were abolished after independence, the Oswals and similar communities abandoned such
rigorous standards of purdah (Mehta 1982:140–44, 152).

Hindu women of the higher jatis wore a blanket-like shawl on
occasion, especially when traveling. It was about as all-covering
as the Muslim woman's burka. But while the burka is still much
in use, this shawl is now rarely seen. In the Bhopal region, such
wrapping is worn by young Hindu women at certain joyous ritual

events, perhaps as much for protection from the evil eye as from lascivious male stares (Jacobson 1982:104, 107).

The traditional burka is made of cotton, all white or all black, and envelops the wearer cap-a-pie. In recent decades, a new style has become popular among the more affluent and less stringent families. It is the two-piece burka, consisting of a long, sleeveless coat over which a cape, nearly waist-length, is worn. The cape covers the head and has an attached veil which falls over the face and can also be thrown back. This burka style is made of silk or rayon, comes in various solid colors; some are even shaped a bit to suggest a waistline and may be in pastel hues. This newer style is more comfortable to wear and, at least to the casual observer, just as concealing.

While some Muslim women, mainly those of high education and

These stylish women are dressed in traditional burkas made of cotton, usually either black or white.

wealth, now find the burka an intolerable impediment, many more say that it is really a liberating garment which permits a certain freedom of movement not possible without it, allowing them to go out of the house or travel to visit their natal home. Moreover, for poor people it is a hallmark of status. Muslim women who must work in the fields, usually aspire to slip into a burka and be rid of field labor (cf. Papanek 1982 [1973]:10–14; Vreede-de Stuers 1968: 60–61, 86).

Muslim women of the Delhi Pirzadas, like the Hindu women of Meerut, must be particularly circumspect in their own mohalla, the neighborhood where they and their families are known. When a woman gets on a bus with her husband to ride to another part of Delhi, she usually throws back her veil to see better. "When returning, she lowers the veil again as they approach their *mohalla*" (Vreede-de Stuers 1968:87).

There is one kind of public place into which a Hindu woman may enter and a Muslim woman does not. It is the place of worship. Hindu women come to pray and make offerings at the temples where their men go and they may go with them. While they may not be allowed into the inner sanctum, they are not barred, as women, from sacred precincts. A Muslim woman does not usually enter a mosque. While she may, if suitably accompanied and attired, attend fairs and festivals, participate in the women's parts of religious ceremonies, visit local shrines, and make long pilgrimages, she does not participate in the daily congregational worship that is mandatory for Muslim men. Hindus approach the congregation of their Gods singly or as a family. Muslims pray publicly to their single God in congregations of males only. Since the mosque is the central public gathering place for a community's men, it is not a suitable place for women.*

This is not to say that these Muslim women are cut off from

* Muslim women must avoid religious acts, objects, and places during their menstrual periods. Unlike the usual Hindu practice, a menstruating Muslim woman may cook and serve food to her family. But she may not touch a copy of the Koran and may not recite verses from the Koran (cf. Jeffery 1979:110–15).

religious participation. They are typically engrossed with domestic devotions, with performing the women's portions of rituals, with worship at shrines.

In her study of a Muslim village in Pakistani Punjab, Zekiye Eglar (1960) tells of the women's involvement in and direction of gift exchanges between families, especially at weddings. These exchanges, in Eglar's account, are of great importance for family prestige and for village economy. And these transactions are essentially under the control of the women.

Muslim women of rural West Bengal, Lina Fruzzetti tells, carry on parts of the life-cycle rituals and conduct all the rites and worship of the local saints, *pir*. That worship is an important part of their lives. Men share in the beliefs about the powers of the *pir* but do not participate in the worship (1980:192–94). These Muslims separate the functions of their supreme deity from those of the saints in a way that parallels the distinction made by Hindus between their transcendental and pragmatic deities (Mandelbaum 1966; 1970:411–13). Among Hindus, women generally have more to do with the pragmatic supernaturals than do men, but there is not the sharp differentiation in worship by gender that is made by these Muslims of West Bengal.

In their rationale for purdah, Muslims invoke religious reasons much more than do Hindus. The close seclusion of women, in the popular Muslim belief, is a fundamental precept of Islam, ordained in the Koran, and is a universal hallmark of the true Muslim way of life. Muslim teachers and preachers, *Maulvi*, regularly exhort the faithful to safeguard that precious quality of Islam and often admonish their audiences, whether male or female, about derelictions from this essential rule (cf. Vreede-de Stuers 1968:61). In Bangladesh villages, purdah "commands respect in a way that money alone does not, because of its religious connotations, since it is considered good behavior from a religious point of view" (Abdullah and Zeidenstein 1980:56).

For Hindus, purdah is not so integral a part of religion. It is more a matter of social concern for family and caste-group, rather than a principle of religious sanction. Mandates for purdah in Hindu holy writ are not commonly invoked. Hindu religious teachers tend rather to emphasize, especially when addressing women, the scriptural ideal of *patrivrata*, the complete devotion of a wife to her husband.

There are some Muslim scholars who challenge the popular, orthodox view about the Koranic foundations for purdah. Thus Fazlur Rahman, an Islamic modernist, states, "The Quran advocates neither veil nor segregation of sexes but insists on sexual modesty." He cites evidence to show that in Arabia, before Islam, women were a central focus of a man's honor and were subjected to close restraints. Paradoxically, according to Rahman, the Koran aimed to remove certain abuses to which women had been subjected because of excessive preoccupation by men with their honor. Rahman reviews the relevant verses of the Koran and concludes, "there is nothing in these verses that calls for purdah as such" (Rahman 1982:286–87, 290–91; also Papanek 1982[1973]:22–27[305–9]; Jacobson 1976a:169–71). These views may eventually be accepted as valid interpretations and may provide scriptural justification for reforms to come. But they are far from the currently prevailing belief among Muslims.

In the nineteenth century and later, a number of social reformers —Hindu, Muslim, and British—advocated changes in women's status. Their efforts did influence the program of the Indian National Congress and ultimately the Constitution of India. But they had little direct effect on the lives of South Asian women in general.

A Muslim reform movement that did have influence on women's activities was that centered in Deoband, northeast of Delhi. Like reformist drives in other world religions, its proponents preached a return to the true meaning of Islamic scripture, as they interpreted the sacred text. A principal publication of that movement is a 1905 book about women, *Jewelry in Paradise*, by Maulānā Thānawī. The title conveys the author's message to women, that they be less concerned with their actual jewels and more with their real jewels, their good deeds and conduct.

In her lucid study of this book, Barbara Metcalf tells that it has been enormously successful. It is still widely available and has been translated from the original Urdu into many other Indian languages. This book, like the Deobandi movement itself, received greatest acceptance among upwardly mobile Muslims who were attracted to assertively scriptural religion as a mark of respectability (1984:186). Through his teaching and writings for this class, Thānawī became "one of the most influential Muslims of twentieth-century India" (Naim 1984:306).

A central element of Deoband teaching was the restoration of women's rights which, these reformers argued, are inherent in Islamic scripture but which have been eroded over time. They preached that women are not outside of, or irrelevant to, true religion, as was then a popular belief, but are capable of religious fulfillment. Thānawī expounds this thesis, consistently writing that women do have capacity for moral behavior. He argues that this is so despite their inherent shortcomings for right conduct, such as excessive emotionalism, flightiness, loud talk, and lack of due care in protecting their valuables and their honor (Metcalf 1984:191).

The book urges women to develop their moral capacities by engaging fully and conscientiously in the rituals prescribed for them. Thānawī advocates that women be literate and educated in Islamic law. A woman so schooled can better perform her wifely duties, improve herself, and, importantly, advance the status of her family. A literate woman can enhance her own and her family's respectability. She will not violate seclusion through clandestine correspondence. "Rather than compromise seclusion she can preserve it, for she can communicate with her distant relatives without going to any outsider" (Metcalf 1984:192).

Thānawī's recommendations for some education for girls and for greater involvement in religious pursuits by women struck a responsive chord among those Muslim men who aspired to better economic and social status under twentieth century conditions. He pointed them in directions in which they wanted to go, provided scriptural reasons they could readily accept.

But in other matters concerning women, Thānawī and his followers stood fast by old ideas and practices. The ideal qualities of a woman, as portrayed in the book, include such virtues as generosity, hard work, keeping eyes lowered in modesty, and being grateful for even the smallest blessing. A woman must learn "above all to relate to her husband as she related to God, with obedience and gratitude." If he should mistakenly treat her as an equal, she must check him, presumably with suitable tact. A woman's first obligation is to know her own subordinate place in the hierarchy that, Thānawī says, pervades both religious and social realms. These reforms did not depart widely from the traditional mold. They did help in a process of change that was parallel to processes which were going on in other South Asian groups (Metcalf 1984:190–94). That process has continued among Muslims, though far too slowly in the view of Muslim women active in the feminist cause.

As we have noted in the Preface, when Thānawī was urged to write a comparable book for men, he replied that, apart from some details, the existing book served both sexes equally well (Metcalf 1984:190). He apparently appreciated that a guide for the conduct of one sex also provides, at least implicitly, a model for the other sex as well.

On certain matters concerning women, the Koran is quite explicit and less open to formal reinterpretation, though such Koranic rules have been quite malleable in actual usage. These include marriage, divorce, polygyny, and inheritance. The marriage bond in Islam is essentially a civil contract with religious connotations, rather than a religious sacrament (Carroll 1982:280). Divorce is formally easy for a man to accomplish by Muslim law, but is not particularly common practice among these Muslims (Ahmed 1976b:xxvi; S. A. Husain 1976:143–50). Polygyny is costly to maintain and is most common in cases where the first wife proves to be barren (cf. Ahman 1976b:xxvi; Lambert 1976:54; Saiyal 1976:258; Aziz 1979:66).

The Koran also lays down that a daughter is entitled to inherit a share in her natal family's property equal, in most instances, to half a son's share. One consequence of this law is said to be the tendency among Muslims to arrange marriages between two whose families are already closely linked. In that way a daughter's share does not go to another set of kin and so does not dissipate her family's resources. Business enterprises, as well as lands, are subject to fragmentation if daughters are married into distant families. Indeed, one reason given for putting girls into strict purdah at or before their puberty is to prevent any possibility that a girl may attract suitors unsuitably remote from the family's interests (Vreede-de Stuers 1968:28; Rahman 1982:297–98; Papanek 1982[1973]:41–42[321]; Jacobson 1976a:206).

As we have noted, however, Muslim women, like Hindu women, are reluctant to claim their legal inheritance rights lest that impair the cherished, benign relations with their brothers. Yet these rights are scriptural and ancient for Muslims while they are not for Hindus, and they are weighed in marriage considerations among Muslims as they normally are not among Hindus. Hence Muslim families generally prefer, other things being equal, to arrange a marriage for a son or daughter to a spouse who is already within the trusted circle of kin and friends. The common preferences in many (not all) Muslim groups is for the marriage of cousins, the children of two brothers or of a brother and a sister.

There is a particularly high incidence of such marriages among the Zikri Baluch, fishermen of coastal Pakistan. In a sample of 171 marriages, 64 percent were between actual first cousins. Special environmental, economic, and sectarian conditions make for this unusually high proportion, but these marriage arrangements are based on the general Muslim inclination for unions between the children of siblings. There is a belief that "it is 'shameful' to give your women to strangers or outsiders" (Pastner 1979:33, 43).

Further reasons appear in the study by Veena Das of marriage preferences as reflected in Pakistani Urdu fiction. In these fictive but not unreal narratives, the right of first refusal in arranging the marriage of a girl rests with the siblings of her parents. The claims of the father's siblings have priority over those of the mother in contracting a girl's marriage to one of their sons. Das finds that a marriage between the children of two brothers symbolizes that the fraternal relations are "harmonious and free from strife." This is particularly important because brothers are co-heirs, and their relations may become embittered about the division of their inheritance. The union of their children is thought to help ease the potential for hostility between them. There is little or no such potential for strife between a brother and sister, and a marriage between their children reinforces what is supposed to be, and usually is, a mutually supportive relationship (Das 1973:37–39). Presumably, the husband's mother becomes a more sympathetic mother-in-law to the young wife because she is also her father's sister.

Muslims, like Hindus, prize the bond between brothers and also fear for its fragility. Hindus bar marriages between the children of brothers. Such unions fall within their incest taboo and would clash with the northern Hindu concept of innate opposition between consanguines and affines. The marriages would create the contradiction of turning brothers, the closest of consanguines within a generation, into distanced affines. Hindus of these regions also prohibit the marriage of a man to his mother's brother's daughter although many Hindu groups of South India prefer just that arrangement. They too tend to favor strengthening the family through close-in marriage.

Muslims and Hindus differ in certain kinship usages, even though in a particular locality the two may have quite similar kinship terminology (cf. Aziz 1979:95). Hindus generally place greater emphasis on solidary obligations among those related by patrilineal descent, as in a lineage. Lineages are exogamous and are commonly traced through four or five generations. Hindu purdah practices, as we have seen, point up the separation between consanguines of one lineage and their affines from other lineages (Vatuk 1982:100). Muslims, by contrast, place more emphasis on the individual's network of kinship ties, traced through both mother and father, with the more intimate kinship affiliations formed at a family's discretion (cf. Jacobson 1970:87, 166–68, 180; 1976a: 207–8; Aziz 1979:119–20; Pastner 1982:170).

All these disparities between Muslims and Hindus in matters of gender are manifest in even greater degree among Muslims of northwestern Pakistan and of neighboring Afghanistan. These are quasi-tribal societies, different in important ways from other Muslims of South Asia. They are prone to internecine conflict and inclined to brute violence. The conflicts include frequent, sometimes open, friction between husband and wife. A man's concern with his personal honor is typically on hair trigger. His response to perceived slight, even from close relatives, is apt to be prompt and violent.

One of these societies is that of the Pukhtun of Swat, as described by Barth (1965) and by Lindholm (1982). The Pukhtun live in high valleys among the mountains of northernmost Pakistan.

To be respected, a Pukhtun man should be determinedly individualistic, fiercely jealous of his personal honor, highly competitive for status, and ever alert to challenge anyone whom he senses as a threat to his own social position. A common enmity occurs between the sons of brothers. As close consanguines, these cousins stand together in some circumstances, but quarrels among them are common, especially about the division and uses of their inherited lands. "A man whose cousin has become wealthy and powerful will feel pressure to pick a fight with him to display his own strength" (Lindholm 1982:74). Under such personal pressures, a lineage is not a stable group with strong claims to loyalty. There is only one claim which commonly rallies lineage members to united effort; it is for vengeance to redeem the murder of a lineage member.

A Pukhtun typically sees his social world as split between his allies and his enemies. Alliances are made by individuals rather than by kin groups. A man "has a choice of enemies and allies and joins or wars with his cousins according to his own perception of advantage" (Lindholm 1982:82). Alliances are often fluid and fleeting. A Pukhtun may abruptly shift his support to the party of a former enemy if he senses that his honor has been impugned by an ally, perhaps only because that erstwhile ally has become more powerful than the man can brook. Because loyalties are apt to be so tenuous, symbols of loyalty to a patron or ally must be constantly demonstrated (ibid., 215–16). A man's most certain allies in this struggle of each against all are his father and brothers, and even they are not always trustworthy (ibid., 66–67).

Solidary relations, whether of factions, patron-client, or lineage, can be subordinated to a man's sense of his personal honor. "For a Pukhtun, honor lies in vengeance, not in keeping a trust." Confrontation is sought because a man "finds his identity in struggle" (ibid., 84, 89). Among the more powerful families, a feud must be carried through to its bitter conclusion, which may mean the ruin of both opposing leaders. Any man who loses all his land is no longer reckoned as a full Pukhtun; he becomes a laborer and thereby forfeits respect and honor (ibid., 74, 109).

The possibility of such dire outcomes does not usually deter struggles. Contestants typically feel that submission is deeply shameful and a man of honor should carry on his struggles no matter at what cost to his kin and community. As one elder told Lindholm, "Thank Allah, I have many enemies" (ibid., 15).

Similar sentiments are reported from a village of Jat Muslims in Hafizabad district in Pakistani Punjab. Inayat Ullah, himself from a village of the locality, writes that the social goal of Jat Muslim individuals and families is to be powerful enough to help one's friends and awe one's enemies. "A person who has no enemy, whom nobody fears and nobody obeys, is a worthless person" (1958:171).

A Pukhtun woman's life is not as permeated with violence as a man's often is, but she lives within the same aura of conflict. Purdah is very strict by any standard. A woman who violates purdah, say by speaking to a man outside her household, is liable to be severely beaten. Purdah is an emotional matter, "one which lies close to the heart of every Pukhtun" (Lindholm 1982:218).

A girl is typically favored by her father, held and cuddled by him (allegations of incest are a frequent subject of gossip). As a woman she has life-long, compassionate relations with her brothers. Her relations with her husband "tend to be warlike." While she must be duly deferent and subordinate to him in behavior, she may have no compunction about reviling him and all his ancestry in the hearing of the children and of anyone else who may be within earshot (ibid., 129, 130, 143).

Men have a very low opinion of womankind, sisters and mothers excepted. They do not talk about women, or talk much with them.

Women voice complaints against all men, brothers and fathers presumably excepted, as being bad and cruel. A woman is loyal to her natal lineage, not to that of her married home. If she is murdered, her brother, not her husband, must take vengeance on the killer. In their married households, "women are essentially strangers in an enemy camp." They have little influence on the men of the family, although they have the considerable power to humiliate them (ibid., 126–27, 148–49).

In some respects, male-female relations among the Pukhtun and similar groups of this region seem to be savage caricatures of gender patterns followed elsewhere in the north of the subcontinent. But the basic features are broadly similar to those we have noted for both Hindus and Muslims—the seclusion and deferential behavior of women; the separation of men's public space from women's domestic space; the importance and the fragility of the bond between brothers; the deep, durable affection between sister and brother; and the tight link between woman's conduct and man's honor.

The Pukhtun, like other South Asian Muslims, emphasize the distinction between trusted insiders and untrustable outsiders, but place even less trust in mercurial insiders and look for more active hostility from outsiders. The masculine ideal is that of a "strong, lonely man struggling against all others for survival and personal honor" (ibid., 112, 160). That sense of honor is a prickly one. Much of a man's life, Lindholm observes, is spent in trying to prove his superiority to his brothers and his other compeers. He typically has a high opinion of his own merit, yet lives with a constant fear of humiliation (ibid., 188, 205). It tends to make him trigger-happy, all the more because he builds his honor through struggles with his enemies. Enemies are thus required for honor; submission to an enemy is a great blow to honor. A man does not reckon himself defeated, battered though he may be, so long as he can issue signals that he has not submitted, that he carries on the fight. The fights are more desperately waged because, as we have noted, a man who loses all his land is wiped out as a true Pukhtun, all honor spent (ibid., 74, 109).

A man's honor hinges on the conduct of the women of his family as much among the Pukhtun as it does throughout the purdah zone. But while Pukhtun women are closely confined to the household, schooled to subordinate status and deferent demeanor, they, too, are personally independent, are not servile, and are quick to lash out against infringement on what they consider to be their rights. Lindholm tells of a woman who found that her husband had sold, without her permission, a cow that her father had given to her. She loudly insulted him and his lineage, tore off his shirt and fought until he knocked her down. Such fights are the common stuff of domestic drama, and "a man who does not beat his wife regularly will be abused by both men and women (including his wife) as a man with no penis" (ibid., 145).

Gender relations among the Pukhtun and others of the region are far from typical of South Asian Muslim practices. But they do illustrate, in magnified degree, some of the differences between Muslim and Hindu versions of purdah.

Both versions agree that women should be much more restrained in their movements and constrained in their conduct than are men. In both versions women are banned from participation in public affairs of the traditional kind. Both assume that a woman must be protected from and must vigilantly shield herself against strangers outside the home. Both are sensitive to potential dangers to the coherence of a joint family from the junior wives. Similar variations according to age, region, class, and education occur in each. Under each regime there is a reciprocal relation between purdah and izzat, between women's seclusion and men's honor.

Muslims, as already noted, tend to put more emphasis on the danger to women from strangers outside the household circle of trust. Hence, they maintain the use of the burka, the curtained conveyances, the placing of girls in purdah at menarche or before. Family elders have some choice about who comes into the household circle. The circle may include affines and friends, as well as a selection of maternal and paternal kin.

Hindus of the northern regions appear more sensitive to dangers to family and honor from within, from the junior wives and their natal relatives. So they are more insistent about veiling and avoidances within the home. They premise an inherent opposition between the family that gives a woman in marriage and the family that receives her. They require that bride and groom come from different villages and a wife conducts herself much differently in her natal home and village than she does in her married place. A family's affines cannot be its intimates. Muslims favor close-in marriages as between the children of brothers. Hindus forbid such cousin marriages; a Hindu bride comes into her husband's family as a stranger. Moreover, Muslims believe that purdah is divinely ordained; for Hindus purdah is more a societal concern than a religious commandment.

Having looked at variations on the shared themes about gender held by Hindus and Muslims, we will next compare the common themes with gender practices in other parts of the world.

CHAPTER 6

Comparisons and Change

PURDAH IN GLOBAL PERSPECTIVE

Viewed in broad human perspective, purdah is one variety of the social avoidances and distancings that are found, in greater or lesser degree, in many societies. The avoidance of certain kin, such as a person's affines of the other sex, is generally a means of mitigating social tensions among people who cannot evade close proximity yet are cast in roles of potential conflict or of social ambiguity. Veiling is both a separation and a conjunction, a way of keeping social distance while still acting together in the same social enterprise (cf. Radcliffe-Brown 1952: 103–4; Murphy 1964).

Some of the characteristics of purdah are widely found among the peoples of the world. The global incidence of certain features is discussed by Sherry Ortner and Harriet Whitehead in their introductory chapter to the volume *Sexual Meanings* (1981). They give an overview of anthropological studies of sex and gender, using the former term as having more to do with biological givens, the latter more with what is construed culturally.

They write that "in every known society, men and women compose two differentially valued terms of a value set, men being *as men*, higher" (Ortner and Whitehead 1981:16; also see Rosaldo 1974; Ortner 1972). A corollary to this is the finding that, nearly everywhere, men control the public domain where universalistic interests are expressed and managed while "nearly universally, women are located in or confined to the 'domestic domain' charged with the welfare of their own families." Other oppositions like this domestic/public pair, are also widely known, such as nature/ culture and self-interest/public good. They are all derived, Ortner and Whitehead state, from the same idea. It is that the sphere of men's activities encompasses the sphere associated with women and is "for that reason" accorded higher value. Men control the broader social groups while women are confined to the subunits being controlled (Ortner and Whitehead 1981:7–8; Ortner 1972).

Further, a man tends to be characterized in terms of such role categories as elder, warrior, or statesman, which have little directly to do with women, while a woman tends to be defined in terms of her relationship to men, as mother, sister, or daughter. Citing a study by Gayle Rubin (1975) the authors note "the (universal) fact" that men have certain rights in their female kin which women do not have, either in themselves or in men (Ortner and Whitehead 1981:8, 11).

These generalizations may be debated as to details and scope, but they are not unexpected in substance. More novel is the finding that what is most important "for the cultural consideration of gender in any given society are the structures of prestige" (ibid., 12).

In another paper of this volume, Ortner writes that a society's prestige system defines "the ultimate goals and purposes of life for actors in that society." What people do to acquire and sustain high prestige is indeed the enactment of the dominant values of their society. Ortner continues, "I ask first what men (for it is usually their prestige system) are trying to do in their societies, and then how that project hinges on the organization of their relations with women" (Ortner 1980:361).

The general sources of "status or prestige" are listed by Ortner and Whitehead as including command of material resources, political might, personal skill, connection to kinship, and other advantageous networks. To transpose "raw" power into "cooked" esteem there has to be effective use of these assets, conjoined with

Men control the public domain, while women are
most often confined to the domestic domain.

at least a modicum of largesse and concern for the public good. Ancestral reputations of high status become the birthright heritage of particular lineages within a society and serve to solidify, in some cases to rigidify, the order of social rank. Prestige hierarchies are, by and large, male games, these authors note, from which women are excluded. Yet a man's ranking in the prestige order and that of his group are closely linked to the conduct of the women (ibid., 12–15, 19, 21).

In sum, these authors find that women are everywhere undervalued in relation to men; men are usually defined in terms of role categories, women more often in terms of their kinship ties to men; men have rights in women which women do not have in men; concerns about prestige and honor are dominant forces in men's social behavior; and a man's prestige is importantly dependent on the behavior of the women closely related to him.

Women's conduct is, therefore, shaped by considerations of men's status; a group's inherited high status requires continuation of the appropriate behavior by the women of the group; the status and the standards are explained through a legitimizing ideology. Note that the characteristic features of purdah and izzat among the peoples of the northern subcontinent are quite congruent with all the features of gender and prestige which Ortner and Whitehead find to be universal among humankind.

One element of gender, according to Ortner, occurs in hierarchical state societies rather than in simpler, tribal ones. It is the close guarding of a daughter's virginity. The requirement that a girl be a virgin at her wedding appears "throughout virtually all hierarchical societies." Ortner also finds that in no pre-state society do people link female virginity and chastity to the honor of the group (Ortner 1981:400; 1978:23). While this statement about all pre-state societies may be questioned, it is true that a girl's virginity before her marriage is as highly prized by the peoples of the purdah zone as it is in any other hierarchical society.

Differences among several world areas are noted by Ortner and Whitehead. They remark that Mediterranean peoples (and, we may add, the people of the South Asian purdah regions) have highly complex and explicit views on the nature of gender, concepts that are used to organize and define many other spheres of life. The peoples of Northern Europe, by contrast, have less highly elaborated notions of gender and these "do not seem to operate as master organizing principles" in other activities (Ortner 1981:6). Ortner also contrasts gender patterns in Southeast Asia with those of North India (and, in our terms, of those of the whole purdah zone). Among the peoples of Southeast Asia, she finds that marriage does not carry the great social importance that it has in North India. Not much wealth is transferred at marriage; women do inherit land and other valuables. A person's kinship bonds are formed through both mother's and father's kin. Which are more important depends primarily on whether a person lives among the father's or the mother's kin. The preferred kind of marriage is between a man and woman who are already linked by kinship or neighborhood.

In Southeast Asia, unlike North India, a woman's consanguineal kinship ties are more important to her than are those she acquires through marriage; divorce is generally easier for women and more frequent than in India (Ortner 1981:399–400).*

If the global comparisons discussed in this chapter prove to be substantially correct (and I suspect that they will), they provide a framework for assessing South Asian purdah. In certain aspects, purdah values and practices are like the beliefs and behavior about gender that are common to most of humankind. Other aspects of purdah are characteristic of hierarchical state societies rather than of simpler, less stratified societies. Still others are shared by peoples in a large sector of the world, not only of the northern parts of the subcontinent but of regions reaching across Southwest Asia to the lands around the Mediterranean.

FROM COX'S BAZAAR TO CASABLANCA

During my army service in World War II, I was stationed briefly at Cox's Bazaar, a town near the boundary between Burma and British India, now between Burma and Bangladesh. It is also the divide between the peoples, cultures, and languages of South Asia and those of Southeast Asia. That divide was then apparent on the main street of Cox's Bazaar. Along one side were the shops and stalls of the Bengalis, mostly Muslims. On the other were the stalls and huts of the Burmese, mostly refugees from the Arakan coast of Burma.

I was struck by the difference in the comportment of the women. Bengali Muslim women were scarcely seen in the bazaar, except as figures in burkas moving about quietly, or as poor vendors sitting silently beside their trays of fruits and vegetables. The Burmese

---

* Stanley Tambiah makes a similar distinction, particularly in dowry and women's rights, as between the cultures of India on the one side and those of Sri Lanka and Burma on the other. He views the practices of the latter as a "weakening" of a basic Indian pattern (Tambiah 1973:159). Ortner's formulation is broader and more apposite for our purposes.

women were at center stage of their side of the street, loudly hawking their wares, bargaining vigorously with customers, and chatting with passers-by. Occasionally, one would light up a fat Burmese cheroot.

Not long after, I received orders to proceed to Washington by first available air transport. Within two days, I found myself in Casablanca in Morocco where I had been displaced on the plane by higher ranks. During the wait for the next available transport, I walked around in Casablanca and was impressed by how similar the conduct of women there was to that of the Bengali Muslim women in Cox's Bazaar, some 7,000 miles away, and how different both were from the demeanor of the Burmese women across the street from the Bengali Muslims.

Other anthropologists have noticed similarities to purdah in the Middle East, North Africa, and parts of Mediterranean Europe (e.g., Jacobson 1970:206–9; Pastner 1972:250–52; Sharma 1980:204; Miller 1981:24; Papanek 1982[1973]:26–27[308–9]; Saiyal 1976: 242–44). To illustrate such parallels between the peoples of the Middle East (including North Africa) and those of the purdah region of South Asia, we draw examples from a few contemporary monographs, articles, and surveys.

A salient theme in the lives of many of these peoples is the central importance of gender conduct and values. "Certainly few objects in Middle Eastern society are as charged with meaning and strong feeling for the native and stranger alike as is the veil." This comes from the overview by Daniel Bates and Amal Rassam (1983:212) who go on to say that the veil symbolizes, for the great majority, the Islamic ethos about sexual morality and modesty.

Veiling or covering within the household is done in much the same way in North Yemen as in Muslim South Asia. Thus, Carla Makhlouf describes the use of the "indoor veil" by women of affluent families in San'a, capital of North Yemen. A woman there veils herself from her husband's brothers, his father, and any other man she may encounter within the home. However, she does not veil before her husband, her own brothers and father, and any other man forbidden as a possible marriage partner for her (1979:30).

Women's veils and cloaking garments may be invested with political as well as religious meaning. After the Iranian revolution of 1979, revolutionary guards patrolled the streets to warn or jail a woman whose dress did not conform to the ruling politicoreligious standards. News reports of November 1981 from Egypt told that two of the assassins of President Sadat testified that a principal reason for killing him was that he had "disobeyed God's order that women should stay at home and because he had made fun of the (women's) veil." Some family elders of South Asia also see the uses of veil and headscarf, gauzy though they may be, as the steely symbolic linchpin of the social order they cherish.

The traditional separation of living spheres between the public domain of the men and the more private, domestic domain of the women is sharply maintained over much of the Middle East. Fatima Mernissi puts it succinctly for Morocco: "Muslim sexuality is a territorial one ..." (1975:81; see also Bates and Rassam 1983:212).

Another parallel is in the easing of some purdah restrictions when a South Asian woman is away from her village or city neighborhood and the retightening when she returns to the environs of her home. A similar shift is reported on a more cosmopolitan level. When Saudi women of wealthy families are in Europe, they may dine in public, drive cars, even dress much as do women of comparable wealth. But when they return to their homeland they resume the strict Wahabi regimen of seclusion (Bates and Rassam 1983:219).

Saudi officials vigorously protested the television documentary of 1983, "Death of a Princess." But there was no denial that this sanction exists, that a woman who has besmirched family honor has sometimes been put to death by her close kin. Case histories of such deaths recorded from the Middle East are much like the case reported from a Hindu family in a village near Delhi (Antoun 1968:684; Kressel 1981; R. S. Freed 1971).

The reasons given through the Middle East for the seclusion and exclusion of women are like those given in South Asia. They are to protect women when outside the home and to protect family and society from women's disruptive influences within.

As in South Asia, the control of a woman's sexuality is inextricably linked to the honor of the men of her family and group. Honor seems as central and emotional a matter for many men of the Middle East as it is for many in the purdah regions. The sources of men's honor as listed by Bates and Rassam are quite the same, including ancestors, piety, generosity, and the proper use of wealth and power. And as in the case of izzat in South Asia, "the most fundamental and universal component of a male's honor in the Middle East . . . is closely tied to the sexual behavior of his womenfolk" (Bates and Rassam 1983:216–17).

To hold that women are weak and vulnerable and yet powerful enough to pose a threat to the honor of men and the integrity of the group may seem contradictory to foreign observers. Carla Makhlouf notes that this apparent contradiction is symbolized by the use of the veil and suggests that the veil "represents— and conceals—contradictions which lie at the core of all cultures: purity and pollution, good and evil, strength and weakness, communication and alienation" (1979:83). Perhaps a Yemeni man, like one of similar belief in South Asia, would proffer a simple resolution. Yes, women are weak in physical strength and in self-control, but they are strong in the disruptive potential of their inherent sexual magnetism.

Consequently, as men of both areas believe, a man should be ever alert to guard the women close to him; he must be keenly sensitive to slights against them or against other components of his honor. Males outside the home circle are temptable; when they yield to temptation they become adversaries. Against their challenge, a man must counter with riposte that is suitable, prompt, and effective (cf. Eickelman 1981:152–53). Defeat is not necessarily dishonorable, but submission to an enemy is. A true man should carry on the fight to rectify a slight until he feels that his peers accept that his honor has been restored and thereby increased.

This standard of manly and womanly conduct is widely acknowl-
edged throughout the Middle East, but is interpreted and enacted
in many different ways. Some of the major axes of difference are, as
in South Asia, according to criteria of class—economic, social, and
educational. Among settled and urban groups, the wealthier and
politically powerful families of a locality tend to be more stringent in women's seclusion than are the poorer and less powerful
families (Patai 1969:117; Eickelman 1981:145–46; Bates and Rassam 1983:218). Stricter seclusion of women is generally a mark
of higher status. Status competition is pervasive; one study shows
that it is rife even among the inhabitants of a slum neighborhood
in Cairo. When a formerly poor family becomes able to afford to
keep the women in greater seclusion, they commonly do so. Pas-
toral nomads and tribal groups, however, set much less store on
veiling and separate women's quarters, although they too accede
to the theme of seclusion and exclusion.

Education, particularly the secondary and higher education of
girls, has become a major influence for change. Reasons for educating women seem to be much the same in the Middle East as
in South Asia. Once educated, a woman tends to take a different
view of her lot in life and is inclined to be more independent in
her conduct than are noneducated women. As in South Asia, as
newly affluent families and groups take on stricter observances,
those with education in the western mode slough off some of these
customs (Eickelman 1981:148; Bates and Rassam 1983:225).

Another set of resemblances lies in women's perceptions and
personalities. The view from inside the domain of women in the
capital of North Yemen is well depicted by Carla Makhlouf. These
are women of wealthy, élite families, who are as formally dependent on men, as closely sequestered as are any in the area.

They spend most of their daily life in the company of women.
They gather almost daily in women's parties for which they dress
up and at which they enjoy music, eating, dancing, and the taking of *qat*, the Yemeni national narcotic. Theirs is a separate,
and in some respects an autonomous, domain from which men
are excluded as much as women are excluded from men's affairs.

Makhlouf suggests that in this and in other Middle Eastern societies, there is a distinctive female view of the social world which
exists side-by-side with the reigning male view. In women's songs
and stories the "general tone is one of satire and ridicule towards
males." They tell how men are fooled by women (1979:24–25, 34,
43–46).

Veils are not straitjackets. Behind their veils, these women of
San'a can manipulate their dress and gestures to show personal
style and individual purpose. In San'a as in South Asia, women
have much influence over the grave and gravid process of arranging
marriages (Makhlouf 1979:32, 35–37, 41–44). Similar examples of
women's influence and ability to manipulate men and situations
are cited from various parts of the Middle East (Eickelman 1981:
141–67; Bates and Rassam 1983:231–33).

Such influence and self-assertion, however, can only occur
within the confines set by men and male dominance. And the
impression of women's personality traits that emerges from Makhlouf's inside view quite corresponds to those we have cited from
intimate knowledge of women in the purdah zone. Makhlouf notes
the atmosphere of relaxation that prevails in women's work and
leisure: "San'ani women do not seem nearly as tense or inhibited
as women in some other cultures." They do not harbor feelings
of self-devaluation or consider the veil as a token of female inferiority. They see themselves as active participants, not passive
pawns, in their family affairs. Makhlouf's concluding sentence emphasizes that they are indeed active participants (1979:21, 25, 36,
42, 97).

There are parallels in family constellations. In both areas, sons
are heavily favored over daughters, males over females, from birth
to death. A young wife finds social redemption in bearing sons,
and her emotional investment in her sons is typically intense. A
father is expected to be more distant and formal with his son (cf.
Mernissi 1975:69–70; Eickelman 1981:143–44; Bates and Rassam
1983:220–21).

These soundings in the ethnographic data indicate that system-
atic comparisons may well demonstrate a common substratum

in matters of gender that underlies the highly variegated cultural landscape westward from Cox's Bazaar to the Atlantic. More comprehensive comparisons may also reveal basic differences as well as further similarities.

A fundamental similarity is that in the Middle East, as in the purdah zone, most Muslims believe that the seclusion of women is a central, inextricable feature of their religion. It must be secured if the faith is to be secure. So it tends to be more fiercely defended by Muslims than by others. Still, even among some of the most ardently orthodox Muslims, definitions of seclusion are beginning to change, interpretation of scripture being revised.

RECURRENT PROCESS AND SYSTEMIC CHANGE

People of all world areas are now beginning to alter; some have markedly changed long-established ideas about women and men and their social interplay. These changes can be viewed in a time span of decades and centuries or over the grander time scale of cultural evolution.

In the long view, major changes may be discerned, changes which shift the whole system of a society. New technologies and ideologies can impel people to form new groups and groupings, to fashion fresh cultural forms, to posit new cultural assumptions, to alter former purposes and relationships, including those of gender. What may appear to the immediate participants and observers as momentous struggles may resolve, in long perspective, into a profile of a recurrent process of change. Such processes are part of the necessary, ceaseless churning within a society by which the people, usually unwittingly, keep the system attuned to fluctuations in its internal and external environments. The family cycle and, on a large scale, the rise and fall of caste groups are instances of this process (cf. Mandelbaum 1970:626–59).

Certain systemic changes emerged after the adoption of plow agriculture. Societies which took up that mode of production subsequently changed other parts of their cultures, including their ideas about sex and gender. Thus Ester Boserup (1970) and Jack Goody (1976) have considered the cultural correlations of plow agriculture as it has been carried on over most of Eurasia.

As Goody traces the developmental sequence, plow agriculture generally yields an economic surplus great enough to permit the development of a more complex division of labor, and that makes plow agriculture even more productive. It also leads to population increase and to growing pressure of people on cultivable land. Land becomes a valued, scarce commodity, and those who come to own and control land become the more affluent, more privileged, politically dominant classes. The land-poor and landless fall into the less advantaged, lower-ranking, dominated classes. Those who have the upper hand and upper rank are alert to defend and expand their holdings and to preserve their life-style.

They are therefore greatly concerned, Goody continues, that their property not be lost or dissipated, and so they have keen interest in rules of inheritance and of marriage. Rights of inheritance are endowed upon both females and males; the sons generally are the primary heirs. Daughters are usually residual heirs and receive their share of the family estate as dowry. Daughters must be married only to spouses of equal or higher class status so that family power and possessions are not weakened by affinal relations with poor and lowly persons. Hence, the sexuality of women is tightly controlled, both to prevent misalliance with status inferiors and to keep consolidated the superior resources of the higher classes.

The most effective means for such control is by the segregation and seclusion of women. So women are withdrawn from work outside the household and this in itself becomes an index of superior status. They are then valued more for their reproductive than for their productive capacities, as producers of children rather than as providers of food. All this applies more to the higher than to the lower classes. The poor cannot afford to be much concerned with the seclusion of their women (Goody 1976).

This analysis usefully indicates the social and economic matrix of gender relations, but some of Goody's interpretations do not fit the South Asian circumstances. Dowry, as we have noted, is not there taken as an ante-mortem inheritance settlement on a daughter. Moreover, purdah practices not only favor the cohesions and eminence of the property-owning classes, as Goody emphasizes, but also favor the continued control by males of wealth-generating property. That control continues through current changes in agriculture. Thus, a considerable economic shift toward capitalist modes of agricultural production has occurred in the Punjab in recent years. It has not, at least not yet, lessened the dependence of women on men (Sharma 1980:202, 206, 207).

Yet early Sanskrit texts bear out some of Goody's long-range formulations. Sometime in the first millenium B.C., there came a change from the simpler, earlier Vedic society to the more complex kingdoms of the Epics. This shift appears to have brought on increased restrictions on the conduct of women (Dharma 1949: 69). It is clear from Sanskrit texts beginning about the fourth century B.C. that women of royalty were secluded and those of the higher classes were restricted in their movements. The dependence of women on men is mandated in the ancient Hindu scriptures (Basham 1954:177–83).*

Purdah as known in recent centuries is often said to have been adopted among Hindus as a result of the Muslim conquest of North India. This is supposed to have been done in imitation of the new overlords and as a means of shielding Hindu women from the freebooters. But popular as this notion is, there is little or no firm evidence to support it (cf. Jacobson 1982:86–87). Muslim dynasties did indeed rule over much of the purdah zone for several centuries and Muslim cultural influence was considerable in such matters as government and architecture. But many Hindus rejected conversion to Islam and ignored or were ignorant of Muslim ways. The Muslim example of strict seclusion may have bolstered Hindu

* Some verses from the Laws of Manu (about the second century A.D.), in Basham's version, tell of a woman's proper relation to men. "She should do nothing independently / even in her own house. / In childhood subject to her father, / in youth to her husband, / and when her husband is dead to her son. / She should never enjoy independence . . ./" (Basham 1954:180).

gender practices among the higher groups, but it did not implant them.

A common process of purdah development is illustrated in Carroll Pastner's study of Panjgur Oasis in Pakistani Baluchistan. Only the families of the ruling élite there observed strict purdah until British political domination took hold in the late nineteenth century. After that, the women of the large middle stratum, the Baluch, also took on purdah restrictions. For one reason, greater political stability made possible more permanent settlement. There were enough economic gains for those of the middle group so that they could afford separate house space and the other appurtenances for women's seclusion. In the same period, orthodox Sunni ways won out over those of a previously dominant heterodox sect. There were also more male strangers about from whom the local women should be protected. In this instance, the effects of British rule brought about economic and political conditions that allowed for the widening of purdah practices.

After independence, Pakistani government officials were posted in the oasis. Some brought in their families, and these provided an esteemed reference group for the observance of purdah by local families. Many of the local men took work in far places. "The seclusion of young wives especially is regarded as a means of insuring honor in the absence of the husband" (Pastner 1982:167–70). The shift in this locality follows the now familiar course. As a lower and poorer group prospers, its families take on prestigious traits. Foremost among these in the purdah regions is the observance of stricter purdah, a prime symbol of new affluence and social mobility. The widening of purdah has occurred on this remote oasis, but in other places there is also a move away from traditional purdah among some families, mainly among those who are urban, educated, and wealthy.

In the purdah zone, those families which enact this process of recurrent change also take on practices with great dynamic potential—education, new occupations, and new facets of lifestyle. These link them to systemic changes that are emerging on the subcontinent and in the world. So, in another sense, these families also lead into the long-term changes in matters of gender that have accompanied modern developments in technology, economics, science, religion, and politics.

An example of a group farther along in the modernization process is given in Karen Leonard's account of the social history of the Kayasths of Hyderabad City over more than two centuries. Their homeland is in the region of Delhi and Uttar Pradesh, and their traditional occupations were those of scribe, clerk, and administrative official. In the eighteenth century, some of them migrated south to the Central Deccan state of Hyderabad, where the rulers were of a Muslim dynasty founded by a seventeenth century military governor. The Kayasths quickly adapted to the new governmental regime, and their adaptation to new conditions and life-styles quickened.

Leonard finds the changes in women's roles and status to be a good index of the general pace of modern change in Kayasth life. She discusses several significant changes in the lives of Kayasth women. An indicator of the trend of change is in the shift in the kinds of names given to girls. In the late nineteenth century, women's names were short, almost like nicknames, and were used in conjunction with the appropriate kinship term. From the early twentieth century, girls were given names of wider reference, as for nationalist figures or literary or mythological characters. This reflected new expectations "as parents increasingly viewed their daughters as people whose names might be known and used outside the family, potential participants in public life" (1978:121).

The age of girls at the time of their wedding ceremony has risen from about six in the late nineteenth century (cohabitation did not begin until after menarche) to about twenty in recent years. Education for girls increased greatly along with the rise in age at marriage. In the last century, education was given to some girls through home tutoring, although there was one highly exceptional Kayasth woman who, because of special circumstance, was able to become an ascetic holy person, a *Sanyassin*. She wrote poetry in Sanskrit, was much admired, and attracted a following of devotees (ibid., 247).

Since the 1970s, virtually all Kayasth girls, even from poor families, have gone through elementary school. Families of more affluence have sent many of their daughters to college, "and a significant percentage of the current generation of women is attaining higher academic and professional degrees" (Leonard 1976:122).

In 1900, no Kayasth women of Hyderabad City worked outside the home. Now a considerable number work as teachers (70 of the 102 teachers of the Mathur subcaste are women). Of the Kayasth doctors in the city, 8 percent are women, and Kayasth women are employed in other modern occupations. These developments, Karen Leonard points out, can be related more to family than to individual achievement "for family welfare rather than personal autonomy appears to be the major consideration behind these changes" (ibid., 122).

Changes in the choice of spouses and in negotiating a marriage alliance, have come about, with greater participation by the prospective bride and groom (Leonard 1978:217–84). In the 1880s each of the seven subcastes of Kayasth in the city was quite strictly endogamous. Marriages across subcaste lines were sometimes arranged between families living near one another who were too poor to arrange a proper union for their children within their respective subcastes. By the 1930s, breaches of subcaste endogamy began to be made by families of wealth and education, among whom the criteria of comparable education and affluence outweighed the requirements of marrying within the subcaste. In the same period, the number of "love matches" out of caste began to increase. Though they were and are a very small proportion of all Kayasth marriages and are made more by men than by women, they reflect the trend toward greater independence by the principals in this critical event and away from total control by parents and kin (Leonard 1976:124–25; 1978:270–73).

Other variables which indicate a weakening of parental controls and greater possibilities for women to choose their partners and to plan their own future are noted by Leonard. These variables, too, "center upon the institution of marriage and they measure more radical structural changes in family and caste patterns" (1976:124).

The shifts in social structure which are emerging among these Kayasths are also going on among their caste fellows in North India as well as among educated and affluent groups both north and south on the subcontinent. Their modern education and occupations and their orientations toward newer life choices and group values are bringing about alterations in gender relations as well as in the whole system of their social relations.

CHAPTER 7

Linkages and Overview

How can we now, after this survey of gender relationships, understand Nehru's statement that the progress of India can be and should be measured by the progress of India's women? Similar ideas that the progress of civilizations could be gauged according to the position of women were articulated by some nineteenth-century social reformers, including British administrators and missionaries (Leonard 1976:117). One kind of understanding stems from the condition that sex roles and the patterns of relations between men and women are not only deeply rooted in cultural precepts and individual experiences, but are also closely linked to many aspects of the functioning culture and society. They affect and are affected by forces of the economy, the polity, religion, and the larger society. They are of the stuff of child-rearing and day-to-day human interchange and are not usually susceptible to ready change. So we may take Nehru's statement to mean that a marked improvement in women's status, as he and most educated people in India would gauge improvement, would denote that comparably great advances had also been made in other sectors of national life.

In the long perspective of centuries, such improvements on a broad front, including women's status, are already underway in consequence of the scientific and industrial revolutions and of accompanying political changes. To be sure, the improvements of recent decades may be undone by nuclear catastrophe or national calamities, notably the calamities that would ensue if population growth is not effectively mitigated. Greatly increased education for girls and higher standards in that education are among the most feasible, surest ways of population control in South Asian nations (cf. Mandelbaum 1974: 102–5). If the peoples of the world can avert titanic mishap, and those of South Asia can surmount their particular social and political dangers, the evolutionary course of their cultures and societies seem well set for the kind of changes that have occurred and are occurring in more industrialized societies. Such shifts include advances in women's status, as Nehru would judge such advance.

This is not to say that South Asian women who are in the forefront of the women's movement would want their societies to produce close copies of women's roles in Western nations. Thus Tara Ali Baig emphasizes that improvements in women's status should not produce the kind of women's liberation that is the goal of feminist activists in Western societies. She adds that change in women's status and in Indian society generally "may be taking place at a pace faster than perhaps we realize. The Indian woman is part of this process, too. With the wisdom gleaned from centuries of discipline and self-sacrifice, she has something positive to contribute today to the search for a solution to the age-old man/woman relationship" (Baig 1976:251). Rama Mehta notes that educated women in India generally want to retain certain of the traditional values of Indian family life and women's roles, an inclination that we have previously noted in other studies. Doing so often entails major personal conflicts in reconciling the ideas gained through their education and the traditional precepts about women's conduct.

In interviews with fifty educated Hindu women, Mehta found that they distinguished modernization from Westernization in their own conduct and the ways of their peers. They were "alarmed by the rapid spread of Western ideas in the élite groups." They were concerned with the problem of adopting the beneficial aspects of Western culture without being "infected by its injurious aspects." The difference between being Indian-modern and Indian-Western is shown in attitudes toward divorce. If a divorce is sought by an educated woman because of extreme provocation, it is condoned, "but if the separation is for a lesser reason, a woman is condemned" (Mehta 1970:205).

It may be that with the strong leadership of women activists in India, the status of women in Indian society will be advanced more rapidly than will modern shifts in other sectors. But some writers sound less optimistic. Thus Muriel Wasi finds that the great mass of Indian women are still abysmally backward, and "this indeed is the main reason why India moves so slowly in the total process of modernizing herself" (Wasi 1971:10). That is all the more true for the peoples of the purdah zone, among whom the traditional standards for women's conduct are so closely bound to central concerns of men's strivings. A further meaning is that once significant improvements in women's lot have been made many other social improvements, as in family planning, will necessarily follow. So an expansion of women's roles and opportunities is both index to and means of implementation for better conditions throughout a society.

To review our examination of the theme of purdah-izzat and to link some of its parts and ramifications, we begin with the beginnings noted in the preceding chapter. The patterns of purdah were instituted, our sketch indicates, as a result of a change in the system of society that was initiated with the introduction of plow agriculture about four millennia ago. This more efficient mode of production eventually was adopted through most of the subcontinent and provided the economic base for specialized division of labor, states, cities, and the other appurtenances of civilization.* Cultivated land became valuable, inheritable property, and those

---

* Some peoples of South Asia did not initially develop in civilizational ways. They lived in hill and jungle lands that were geographically remote and culturally isolated from the main centers and currents of Indian civilization. They remained organized as tribal societies, more egalitarian and less stratified than those of the civilized mainstream. As of 1985, there were about fifty-five million people on the subcontinent who were classed as tribals. Tribal women still had much less formal subordination and more independence than did women of more highly stratified groups in South Asia (cf. Mandelbaum 1970:573–92).

who owned such land or other production resources became the upper classes of stratified societies.

In South Asia, the hierarchical relations between classes that are characteristic in civilizations became elaborated into caste orders. The social and ritual separation between groups became pervasive in social scope and sharpened in cultural degree. Inequality came to be intensified in gender as in general group relations. (The title *Towards Equality* [1974] of the report of the governmental committee on the Status of Women in India indicates the contemporary turning beyond this stage.) All societies are in some respects hierarchical, as in relations between child and adult, and in other respects more egalitarian, as among equally contributing partners in a joint enterprise. In Hindu caste relations, the local social hierarchies were linked to and legitimated by a religious ideology about ritual pollution and purity and their social importance.

When foreign scriptural religions with other ideologies became established in South Asia—Islam, Judaism, Christianity—their adherents, who were mainly converts from Hinduism, retained a principal presumption of caste. It is that most important social interactions necessarily take place between a superior and a subordinate. South Asian groups of high status (those who were materially more powerful or ritually more pure or both) also came to place the great value on female virginity before marriage that, as Ortner and Whitehead tell us, is characteristic of all strongly hierarchical societies. Relations between men and women stand as a prototype of such social ranking, both in the early experiences of the individual and in the assumptions of the group.

The system of caste has remained remarkably stable in South Asia, at least over the past few centuries for which there is relatively good historical evidence. That stability has been sustained in part through recurrent struggles in local caste orders for changes in the ranking of particular groups. Fierce competition for higher status has commonly been waged within a locality when a lower group prospers and begins to assume the symbols and appurtenances of superior rank. The higher groups generally oppose their aspirations. The challenges were part of a systemic counterchange by which secular power and ritual rank among jatis, "caste groups," were kept in broad parity. Few groups successfully challenged the premises of caste ranking, and the system as a whole remained stable even though particular groups rose or fell in a local order of rank (Mandelbaum 1970:630–35).

While opposing higher groups could fight to block certain of a lower group's mobility tactics, such as owning land or wearing the sacred thread, they could not easily stop them from secluding their women. And though families of the poor cannot meet the costs of keeping strict purdah, the poor as well as the affluent have believed in its merit and in that of the coupled concept of izzat.

The key social concept of izzat encompasses many of the principal motivations and goals of a man and a family in the purdah zone.* And izzat is critically dependent on the conduct of the family's women. Gender standards, according to Ortner and Whitehead, are closely bound to prestige patterns in all societies (1981: 12). If so, those of the northern subcontinent are prime exemplars of such linkage. As we have noted in various contexts, women can put family honor in jeopardy both outside and inside the home. Outside, a woman's conduct must be constrained lest her inherent power of sexual attraction lead her, willingly or unwillingly, into indiscretions that could bring shame and dishonor to her husband and family.

Within a joint family, the wives of the brothers are likely to be seen by the senior men and the senior women as potential threats

---

* The sense of honor among Sikhs was engaged by the tragic events at Amritsar in 1984. When troops of the Indian army shot their way into the Golden Temple of the Sikhs in order to quell what the government judged to be an armed uprising, many Sikhs felt the action to be an intrusion of great affront, a brutal violation of their most sacred precincts. One leader of Sikh organizations in the United States appeared on national television and told of fellow Sikhs who were considering suicide as a way of responding to what they held to be the Indian government's insult to Sikh honor. And when the Prime Minister, Indira Gandhi, whom they considered to be culpable, was assassinated by two Sikh members of her bodyguard, a number of Sikh extremists in New York City came to the United Nations Plaza to dance in jubilation (and before television cameras) at the redemption of their honor.

to the cherished, if fragile and ultimately untenable, cohesion of the family. If and when that cohesion is broken, the power and prestige, the izzat, of its members is at risk. Though many village families and more families of towns are nuclear rather than joint, and domestic interplay within them differs from that in a joint family, similar ideas about a young wife are commonly held by the husband in a nuclear family and by his closest elders.

Perceptions about danger to honor rest on certain assumptions about the nature of man and woman. One is that a woman possesses, before she becomes an older matron, an innate sexual magnetism which men (fathers, brothers and sons excepted) can resist only by force of will and not in all situations. As a man is assumed to have low resistance to a woman's sexual allure, so an unprotected woman is supposed to have uncertain powers of resistance to a man's sexual advances. Another assumption is that a woman is likely to promote her own interests above those of her husband's family and that over time a man is likely to succumb to his wife's influence in diverting him away from his true duty to his parents and brothers.

Each person acquires such cultural assumptions in childhood, either specifically inculcated or generally absorbed from social experience. Both boys and girls, as Sudhir Kakar finds, typically experience a benign supportive, ego-enhancing social environment in early childhood. Girls undergo a difficult shift at marriage, but it is a change for which they have been prepared, and they are commonly treated with special tenderness in the years just before they leave home.

A boy of these regions, as Kakar presents the modal case, experiences a traumatic shock at about age five when he is transposed from the more affectionate domain of the women to the harsher terrain of the men. There his father is a daunting, ambiguous figure who is culturally obliged to keep aloof from him, and yet one who cannot but show signs of affection, or at least concern, for him.

The characteristic consequence, Kakar concludes, is that the boy grows up to be a man who has a good opinion of himself but is unsure enough ("narcissistically vulnerable") so that he must continually try to prove his worth. In his relations with women then, he insists that he constantly be reassured of his superior status. In his relations with men, he navigates his personal course in a society that is hierarchical and in which reaffirmations of superiority-subordination are frequently required. Nonetheless a man typically feels impelled to elevate his status vis-à-vis others, especially those close to him in rank, whenever he senses that it is possible and desirable to do so. This drive to better one's position, when joined in group effort, leads to the recurrent competition to change and elevate group status that, in seeming paradox, has made for historic stability in the systems of society in South Asia.

Not all men are equally set on raising personal or group status. Some men and some groups are content to remain where they are in their social order or are perforce resigned to staying there. But even a man who is content with his social lot may be stimulated to vigorous defensive action when he feels that an upstart individual or a rising lower group threatens to demean his own position by their rise.

A man's efforts to change his and his group's social position do not negate his inclination for hierarchy. He typically wants to improve his status, but not to do away with hierarchical ranking. Achieved social mobility enhances izzat; thwarted mobility efforts do not necessarily mean dishonor; one can resume the struggle another day. Success usually requires entrepreneurial abilities in putting together profitable economic combinations, in creating strong political coalitions and, as the conclusive seal and signet of success, in negotiating prestigious marriages for one's daughters. There is no dearth of entrepreneurs in South Asia.

Women share these perceptions and drives but must confine their direct participation to their own domestic domain. To influence public action, a woman works through the men of her family. Women are schooled from early childhood to signal their subordinate status as females but, as close and qualified observers testify, that does not quench all spark and spirit. For one reason, a woman has typically had some supportive relationships during her childhood and early adolescence. Once she has passed through the

gauntlet of being a new wife and when she bears a child, she se-
cures personal gratifications from various sources, among them extended visits to her natal home. Few women say that their lives are
unruffled, their treatment completely fair, their life scenarios rosy.
But there are as yet proportionately few, and those mainly educated women, who publicly assert that they have been oppressed
as women. In her book *We Will Smash This Prison* (1980), Gail
Omvedt holds that women's consciousness of their oppression is
widespread and is leading to active revolt against such oppression.

Education has been an important vehicle in speeding the systemic social changes that have come about in the wake of the
technological, scientific, and political revolutions of recent centuries. Education itself is part of a recurrent process, taken up first
by higher, wealthier groups as a new source of power and izzat.
At first, many saw education in the Western mode as a means of
gaining employment or preferment under the British; it soon was
developed into a thoroughly indigenous set of institutions. No one
in political authority in South Asia claims that education in their
nation is adequate in scope or quality at any level. Despite major
advances in educational facilities since independence, education
in each South Asian nation is far below the stage envisioned by its
leaders. Yet everyone also knows that education can bring about
great changes in the status and power potentials of individuals
and their groups. Educated people, those with a high school education or more, typically differ from those of lesser education in
such respects as fertility, health, occupation, life-style, and in their
practices concerning gender roles and relations.

Yet, as we have noted, some elements of purdah are retained
among educated urban people. Dowry payments, for one example,
show little sign of diminishing in incidence or amount despite
decades of vigorous attacks against the practice in the press and
legislatures.

In recent years added impetus to anti-dowry efforts has come
from revelations of the deliberate immolation of young women
in order to permit their husbands to gain another bride and her
dowry. Reports of "bride-burning" have appeared on national and

international television and radio and in newspaper and magazine accounts. The usual story is from New Delhi and other cities; it tells of a husband and mother-in-law who are dissatisfied with a young wife and demand more dowry from her parents. If they do not get it, they arrange that the young woman be "accidentally" burned to death in her kitchen. They then arrange another marriage for the man and collect another dowry (Lopamudra 1983).

There have been strong efforts in some Muslim groups, especially in Pakistan, to reinstate practices which many perceive to be properly Islamic. Laws concerning them have been promulgated as an expression of political allegiance and public policy. But political regimes are transitory, political expressions can swiftly change, and neither seems likely to block for very long the emerging changes in purdah patterns.

In 1979, the military government of Pakistan under General Zia ul-Haq instituted a series of political and administrative changes intended to bring about a greater degree of Islamization in the country. These included the altering of some women's rights away from those previously extended along British lines to those indicated by the orthodox Sunni interpretations of Koranic verses and traditional Muslim laws concerning women. Policies for Islamization "promote institutionalized gender inequality based on the concept of distinct social roles for each gender" (Korson and Maskiell 1985:600). Protests by educated Pakistani women induced General Zia to make some conciliatory gestures. In 1980, a new Women's Division was established in the Cabinet Secretariat, designed to "safeguard and advance the position of women in the country." As Anita Weiss writes, women's "status has been simultaneously uplifted by the establishment of the Women's Division yet diminished by the incorporation of some Islamic laws" (1985: 864).

Particularly obnoxious to educated Pakistani women was a proposed new regulation delimiting the right of women to give legal testimony in court. Despite the tight police control over expressions of political opposition, a number of women lawyers and other prominent women staged street demonstrations in 1983 in Lahore and in Karachi. The demonstrators in Lahore were dispersed by police wielding *lathis*, staves. The assault on the women demonstrators was denounced by a few politically diverse groups. But the demonstrations were condemned in many newspapers as being sacrilegious. A group of some one hundred renowned *ulema*, religious leaders, not given to understatement, "have ascribed women's protest against the Law of Evidence as a proclamation of war against God's commands" (Korson and Maskiell 1985: 606).

Women's organizations have challenged the government's interpretation of Muslim law, especially the requirement that acceptable evidence must be given by at least two women in cases where the evidence of one man suffices. Court suits on the interpretation of Muslim law have been brought, and some judges have reserved the right to themselves to decide which of several possible interpretations of Islamic law is the one to be enforced under contemporary social and religious conditions.

Out of the struggle between the educated and resolute women of the social élite and the professionally resolute but legally vague military leaders there may come a new movement in the interpretation of Koranic precepts and traditional law. The politically appealing calls for Islamization may come to be fulfilled in terms of new interpretations, of the kind we have noted being advanced by Islamic modernists like Rahman.

For the women engaged in the travails of these and similar struggles, it is small comfort to know that their efforts are part of the tide of history. But it may be some help if they realize that, long after the General Zias are gone and forgotten, the results of their efforts will continue to benefit the lives of both their countrymen and women.

When we consider purdah-izzat in comparative perspective, some telling cultural links, as well as cultural disparities, become apparent. One comparison is between Muslim and Hindu versions within the purdah zone. Another is within the subcontinent, between gender practices of the north and those of the south. A third comparison traces some similarities between gender roles and relations within the subcontinent with those observed over the Middle East and North Africa. We have only briefly mentioned comparisons with Southeast Asia. All these comparisons should be taken as preliminary formulations, worthy of more detailed examination, especially when more ample anthropological data become available. Gender variations within the purdah zone merit further anthropological study as do comparisons with other regions of the subcontinent.

Muslims and Hindus of the purdah regions share certain elementary ideas about gender. They agree that a woman should be, and should always take care to appear to be, subordinate to the men closest to her. She must be secluded from easy personal interactions outside her home and excluded from public affairs except, as we have seen, for those few women who attain prestigious office and so accrue credit to family and group izzat. Within the household, a woman should signal her acceptance of the reigning hierarchy by frequent flashing of signs of respect. And a man, they also agree, should be zealous about his izzat, hold it in constant concern, and be especially vigilant that the conduct of the women closest to him does not impugn his honor.

From this common base, Muslim and Hindu gender practices diverge. Muslims are even more concerned than Hindus generally are, about protecting their women from outsiders. Hence Muslim women wear the burka, prefer to travel in sight-proofed compartments, and are generally under closer chaperonage when they venture forth. Within the household, a Hindu woman, especially a young wife, seems to be under stricter surveillance than her Muslim counterpart. This is partly because of differences in marriage patterns. These northern Hindus postulate an inherent inequality between two families related through marriage, the bride-givers being inferior to the bride-receivers. They also assume that there is antagonism between the two families. It is as though these Hindus, more than do Muslims, fear the disruptive potential of a wife and her natal kin. Hence they have village exogamy, they bar marriage between two from the same village.

Village exogamy insures that families related through marriage do not live close to each other and that a young wife does not have ready access to her original family. When she does visit them, she alters her conduct. In her childhood home and village she can come out of the connubial closet, can walk about unveiled as she did before her marriage.

Muslims recognize no such inequality and opposition between affinally related families. Indeed, they prefer to arrange marriages between two whose families are already related in kinship or are friendly. The preferred match for a man is with his patrilineal parallel cousin, his father's brother's daughter, a union that is forbidden by Hindu incest taboos. So a Muslim bride does not necessarily come into her new home as a complete stranger and is likely to be on friendlier, less probationary terms with her new relations.

Men's honor is as closely linked with women's conduct among Muslims as among these Hindus, but a Muslim man tends to be more individualistic in the pursuit and defence of izzat. While firm comparative evidence is not as yet available, it seems that a Muslim man is generally less committed than a Hindu typically is, to received networks of kinship and is more concerned about his own choices among kin to be kept close, friends to whom to be loyal, allies to be cultivated.

An example of Muslim individualism carried to a Hobbesian extreme, is that of Pukhtun society in which, if everyone is not quite in a condition of war with everyone, a man's sense of izzat requires him to be frequently at odds with other Pukhtun. Fights among cousins of a lineage are not uncommon.

A Pukhtun best builds his izzat through conflict with other men. In that sense he needs enemies and is likely to find them, if not in one context then in another. Defeat is not dishonorable; acceptance of defeat, submission to an enemy, is. So long as a man carries on his fight, keeps himself concentrated on exacting vengeance, so long does he feel his honor to be unsullied. Resistance fighters in the long struggle in Afghanistan, geographically close and culturally similar to the Pukhtun, seem to have been sustained by a like sense of izzat.

Another difference between Hindus and Muslims is in the perceived relation of gender modes to religion. Muslims hold purdah to be ordained in sacred scripture. While Hindus can find support in their scripture for properly modest conduct of women, they consider purdah to be more a matter of social propriety and family status than of divine decree.

In the twentieth century, the Koranic verses that relate to women were given a fresh interpretation, as we learned from Barbara Metcalf's study (1984), noted earlier, by the influential Indian Muslim writer and reformer, Thānawī. His 1905 guide for Muslim women appealed particularly to a new class of Muslims who were gaining in status and wealth under the British Raj. Thānawī taught that, contrary to what was then a popular Muslim view, women are not lesser breeds without the Law but are endowed with moral sensibilities and are capable of moral conduct. They are relevant to Islam; Islamic rituals and ceremonies are relevant for them. He advocated some education for women in Islamic scripture and law, a recommendation that may have prepared the way for other kinds of education for Muslim girls of affluent families. That the case for girls' education should have been convincingly presented as flowing from a righteous interpretation of scripture is in keeping with the general coherence of Muslim culture and Islamic religion. There were also a number of Hindu writers and religious leaders who advocated higher status for women, in such matters as the remarriage of widows and the education of girls. Their influence was effective mainly within particular castes and reformist sects.

Religion is highly important in the cultures of Hindus as well, but Hindu cultures are not as focused on a single scriptural source, their worship and ways, including gender patterns, not as formally aligned in a single direction. In South Asia, Muslim cultures are more closely knit around holy writ, Hindu societies more centrally concerned with social bonds and obligations.

The advent of television in urban areas has introduced a potentially powerful force for change in social perceptions. It promises to be a culturally leveling force, but it is still much too soon to tell whether it may soften the hard perception of Muslim-Hindu differences or the traditionally received concepts about sex roles and gender relations.

When we shift the axis of comparison to contrast gender traits of the south with those of the north of the subcontinent, still other contrasts in gender practice become apparent. As we have noted, the south is here taken to include the four principal linguistic-cultural regions which are also, by and large, the states of Andhra Pradesh, Karnataka, Tamil Nadu, and Kerala. The north here is what we have called the purdah zone, those parts of the northern subcontinent that include Pakistan on the west through eastern Uttar Pradesh, plus Bangladesh.

In the south as in the north, women are required to conduct themselves with alert modesty outdoors and to show proper respect to elders within the home. But the symbolic displays of modesty and respect are generally less stringent and constant, and concern about them is less central to society and culture. Men of the south are sensitive about their status and are typically highly motivated to improve or defend their status. While the competition for personal and group status is generally keen, it is cast in different terms than izzat, with greater stress on ritual pollution and purity.

The comparison of weddings north and south, discussed above from Pauline Kolenda's study (1984), brings out several sharp contrasts relevant to gender. The rites of the southern group are directed toward easing the bride's transition to another role and family. In the north the bride's trauma of parting is dramatized in ritual and often enough realized in fact.

The northern rites emphasize the inferiority of bride-givers to bride-receivers, an inequality that has small place in weddings in the south. The built-in antagonism between the two families that is assumed in the northern rituals does not appear in the southern. Kolenda sees a principal purpose of the southern rites as promoting the future fertility of the woman, that of the northern ceremony in enhancing the prestige of the men.

A demographic consequence of this, as we noted in discussing

Barbara Miller's findings (1981), is that girl children have higher mortality rates in the north than in the south. Proportionately more female infants and juveniles die in the north because a sick boy usually gets better and longer medical treatment than does a sick girl and because boys, on the whole, probably get better nutrition than do girls from whatever food is available in a family. Families both north and south have a marked preference for the birth of a son as opposed to a daughter. The preference is sharper among groups where dowry payments are great and weigh heavily on the arranging of a marriage. The custom of dowry seems to be more costly for a bride's family of the north than in the south.

An environmental-economic reason for these differences in women's place in the south and the north is suggested by Barbara Miller. Greater rainfall in the southern regions makes possible rice cultivation by the labor-intensive transplanting method. Women provide an important part of the total labor input in this way of growing paddy. Climatic conditions in the northwest, as contrasted with the northeast, favor the growing of wheat as a staple. Women's labor is much less important in the cultivation of wheat than of paddy. "Work makes worth" is Miller's summary phrase and so women occupy higher status where their work is more important economically. It is an interesting, perhaps oversimplistic hypothesis that needs testing, say by studies in Bangladesh and in dry-farming districts of the south.

Technological advances in agriculture, especially as manifested in the green revolution in wheat growing, have not benefitted the status of women, at least in the short-term. Boserup has noted that, in general, with technological improvements in agriculture, men's labor productivity increases, but women's productivity remains relatively static (Boserup 1970:53–57, 220–25). So has it been in the recent development of wheat cultivation. It is the men who now drive the tractors, receive instruction from government change agents, and negotiate for seeds and fertilizers. Women continue to carry head loads and to do the traditional menial tasks, and they get little or no share of the prestige that comes with mastering the new production techniques (Jacobson 1977b:225–

26). In the long run increased income made possible by the green revolution is bringing about more education for girls. Already the age of marriage in the Punjab has risen markedly and education for girls is likely to increase greatly (Mandelbaum 1974:56).

To turn to comparison between south India and the northern purdah zone, the south is predominantly Hindu; Muslims are some 10 percent of the total population of the four states. But in some respects relating to gender, southern Hindu practice is more like that of Muslims than of northern Hindus. Families in the south, as do Muslim families, prefer to arrange close-in marriages between two whose families are already related or are on friendly terms. The Muslim preference for marriage of a man to his parallel cousin, his father's brother's daughter, is taboo in the south, where the preference among many groups is for a woman's marriage to one of her cross-cousins, particularly her mother's brother's son. Village exogamy is not the strict rule in the south as it is in much of the Hindu north.

Eastward of the subcontinent, through Southeast Asia, gender relations are quite different from those of the purdah zone. The formal subordination of women is less marked, their conduct more free. Kinship bonds are based on relations through both matrilineal and patrilineal descent. Marriage is not as pivotal a concern. Sherry Ortner has contrasted gender patterns in Southeast Asia with those of North India in three principal features (1981:398–99). The North Indian emphasis, in her appraisal, is on patriliny, exogamy, and dowry. The Southeast Asian preference is rather for cognatic descent, endogamy, and female inheritance. This contrast holds true for northern Hindus but, as we have seen, Muslims of the purdah regions incline toward cognatic descent, endogamy, and female inheritance (in Muslim law, if not in usual practice). Ortner's formulation of this contrast needs further study and repair.

Westward of the subcontinent, across the broad span of Islamic peoples of the Middle East and North Africa, gender patterns are generally similar to those of the purdah regions and, as to be expected, are particularly like those of the Muslim version of purdah-

izzat. Our comparisons in this direction are only preliminary prob-
ings; further enquiry will doubtless reveal significant differences
in matters of gender within and among these regions as well as
further details about linkages with gender practices on the subcontinent.

Our sampling of surveys and monographs shows that gender concerns are central, sensitive matters throughout these areas as they
are in the purdah regions. Female sexuality is considered a serious
potential danger to men and society. A man's honor, among these
peoples too, is closely linked to the conduct of the women of his
family. The typical constellation of family relations is like that
of South Asian Muslims. Similar also are the reports by women
anthropologists that these sequestered women are not personally
crushed under the weight of restrictions but are generally as lively,
productive, manipulative, and active within their own sphere as
are many of the women in purdah.

Women's seclusion accrues to family prestige, and among these
peoples also the degree of seclusion varies by socio-economic class.
The education of girls is beginning to shift attitudes and practices
concerning gender, slowly for the most part, but quite rapidly in a
few groups. Considerable momentum for change may be building
behind the veils.

Political relations, no less than gender relations, tend to be seen
by devout Muslims in religiously focused light. A man's sense of
honor imbues his political activities just as political developments
arouse his sensibilities of honor. And honor requires, as it does in
the purdah regions, that a man should not submit to his enemies.
One's enemies are, in a sense, the gauge of one's honor, and in
these societies enemies are never far to seek. So men may com-
memorate their defeats, as symbols of refusal to yield, as well as
their victories.* To be sure, pragmatic forces can often deflect even

---

* One television vignette exemplified this spirit for me. It was a news report of
some factional street fighting in Beirut. The camera was situated just behind
several of the fighters who were ducking and dodging, firing their weapons, and
being fired upon. One fighter had only one leg, perhaps the other had been shot

a zealous man's quest for honor. But standards of male honor still influence political as well as family events in the Middle East, as they do in the purdah regions of South Asia.

Finally then, the cultural interpretations of the properties of each sex that are made by any society are complementary. How a woman is expected to behave is linked to how a man is expected to conduct himself as a man. An account of either male or female roles requires a complementary account of the roles of the other sex if it is to be reasonably complete.

Practical problems of fieldwork intervene in the study of gender in the purdah zone. A male anthropologist is usually barred from close observation in the women's domain and long conversations with women. Fortunately, there are now an increasing number of excellent reports by women anthropologists of women's life in these societies. Anthropologists have as yet produced few comparable studies of male roles and men's gender obligations among these peoples.

Gender relations are likely to be linked, as we have noted for purdah-izzat, to the major themes of a culture. This linkage is particularly strong among the peoples of the purdah zone, for whom gender relations command much social concern. In matters of sexual ascription, anatomy is part of one's destiny, physiology a factor in one's fate everywhere. They are all the more so for the men and women of the purdah regions.

We have examined purdah-izzat from several perspectives—deep in cultural time, deep in personality development, broad in pan-human and areal comparisons. We have also noted several major forces that impinge on this gender complex, that of mode of agricultural production as between wet and dry cultivation, that of economic class, that of religion as between Muslims and Hindus, and that of modern education. Any judgments as to which of these sight-lines and forces are the more useful for an anthropological

---

away in an earlier skirmish. He was hopping about vigorously, shooting rapidly, taking cover clumsily. A man of honor, he might have explained, should never consider himself *hors de combat*.

understanding of gender depend on the state of the endogenous development of anthropology and related disciplines, and on the pressure of exogenous factors (cf. Mandelbaum 1982). As anthropologists make their field observations and mull over their findings, new approaches and new topics for investigation are necessarily formulated. Some of them come to be vigorously explored. Future studies of gender may well devote increased attention to such relevant matters as case analyses, event analyses, socialization, life history, and the economic matrix of gender relations.

As for exogenous influences, the recent burgeoning of gender studies, done mainly by women, is itself a result of the vastly increased interest in women's rights and in political movements to upgrade women's roles. These studies, in turn, may well influence the political changes in gender ascription that are being sought. And, as we have noted, gender standards also reach into politics in another way, especially in those countries where a man's honor is still a lively, emotionally powerful concern. Because gender studies investigate universal, pervasive, and potent forces in human life, they command theoretical interest in anthropology. They may also help our understanding of political affairs in those nation-states in which male honor commands homage.

BIBLIOGRAPHY

Abdulla, Tahrunnessa, and S. A. Zeidenstein
  1980 *Village women of Bangladesh, Prospects for Change.* New
         York: Pergamon Press.
Ahmad, Imtiaz
  1976a *Family, Kinship and Marriage among Muslims in India.* Edited
         by I. Ahmad. New Delhi: Manohar.
  1976b "Introduction. Caste and Kinship in a Muslim Village of
         Eastern Uttar Pradesh." In *Family, Kinship, and Marriage
         among Muslims in India,* edited by I. Ahmad, pp. xvii–xxxiv,
         319–45. New Delhi: Manohar.
  1978a *Caste and Social Stratification among Muslims in India.*
         Edited by I. Ahmad. 2d ed. New Delhi: Manohar.
  1978b "Introduction." In *Caste and Social Stratification among
         Muslims in India,* edited by I. Ahmad, pp. 1–18. New
         Delhi: Manohar.
  1981a *Ritual and Religion among Muslims in India.* Edited by
         I. Ahmad. New Delhi: Manohar.
  1981b "Introduction." In *Ritual and Religion among Muslims in
         India,* edited by I. Ahmad, pp. 1–20. New Delhi: Manohar.
Alberuni
  1971 *Alberuni's India.* Translated by E. C. Sachau. Edited by A. T.
         Embree. New York: Norton.
Ali, Mrs. Meer Hassan
  1917 *Observations on the Mussulmans of India.* Edited by
         W. Crooke. 2d ed. London: Oxford University Press. First
         published in 1832.
Antoun, Richard T.
  1968 "On the Modesty of Women in Arab Muslim Villages, A Study
         in the Accommodation of Tradition." *American Anthropologist*
         70:671–97.
Aziz, K. M. Ashraful
  1979 *Kinship in Bangladesh.* Dacca: International Centre for
         Diarrhoeal Disease Research. Monograph Series No. 1.
Babb, Lawrence A.
  1975 *The Divine Hierarchy.* New York: Columbia University Press.
Baig, Tara Ali
  1976 *India's Woman Power.* New Delhi: S. Chand and Co.

Bardhan, Pranab
  1982   "Little Girls and Death in India." *Economic and Political*
          Weekly (Bombay) 17:1448–50.
Barth, Frederick
  1965   *Political Leadership Among Swat Pathans*. London: Athlone
          Press.
Basham, A. L.
  1954   *The Wonder That Was India*. New York: Grove Press.
Bates, Daniel G., and Amal Rassam
  1983   *Peoples and Cultures of the Middle East*. Englewood Cliffs,
          New Jersey: Prentice-Hall.
Beech, Mary Higdon
  1982   "The Domestic Realm in the Lives of Hindu Women in
          Calcutta." In *Separate Worlds*. Edited by H. Papanek and
          G. Minault, pp. 110–38. Delhi: Chanakya Publications;
          Columbia, Missouri: South Asia Books.
Berland, Joseph C.
  1982   *No Five Fingers Are Alike. Cognitive Amplifiers in Social*
          Context. Cambridge: Harvard University Press.
Bertocci, Peter J.
  1974   "Rural Communities in Bangladesh: Hajipur and Tinpara." In
          South Asia: Seven Community Profiles, edited by C. Maloney,
          pp. 81–130. New York: Holt, Rinehart and Winston Inc.
Bhatty, Zarina
  1975   "Women in Uttar Pradesh: Social Mobility and Directions of
          Change." In *Women in Contemporary India*, edited by A. de
          Souza, pp. 25–36. Delhi: Manohar.
  1976   "Status of Muslim Women and Social Change." In *Indian*
          Women: from Purdah to Modernity, edited by B. R. Nanda.
          New Delhi: Vikas.
Bookman, L. M.
  1978   "Hindus and Muslims: Communal Relations and Cultural
          Integration." In *Main Currents in Indian Sociology*, vol. 3,
          Cohesion and Conflict in Modern India, edited by G. R. Gupta,
          pp. 103–27. New Delhi: Vikas.
Boserup, Ester
  1970   *Women's Role in Economic Development*. London: G. Allen
          and Unwin.
Brijbhushan, Jamila
  1980   *Muslim Women in Purdah and Out of It*. New Delhi: Vikas.
Carroll, Lucy
  1982   "Talaq-l-Tafurid and the Stipulations in a Muslim Marriage
          Contract." *Modern Asian Studies* 16:277–309.

Daniel, E. Valentine
1984   *Fluid Signs, Being a Person the Tamil Way.* Berkeley, Los
        Angeles and London: University of California Press.
Das, Veena
1973   "The Structure of Marriage Preferences: an Account from
        Pakistani Fiction." *Man in India* 8:30–45.
Dharma, P. C.
1949   "The Status of Women During the Epic Period." *Journal of
        Indian History* 27:69–90.
D'Souza, Victor S.
1976   "Kinship Organization and Marriage Customs among the
        Moplahs on the South-west Coast of India." In *Family, Kinship
        and Marriage among Muslims in India,* edited by I. Ahmad.
        New Delhi: Manohar.
Eglar, Zekiye
1960   *A Punjabi Village in Pakistan.* New York: Columbia
        University Press.
Eickelman, Dale F.
1981   *The Middle East, an Anthropological Approach.* Englewood
        Cliffs, New Jersey: Prentice-Hall.
Epstein, T. Scarlett
1960   "Economic Development and Peasant Marriage in South
        India." *Man in India* 40:192–232.
Freed, Ruth S.
1971   "The Legal Process in a Village in North India." *Transactions
        of the New York Academy of Sciences,* 2d ser., vol. 33, pp.
        423–35.
Freed, Stanley A.
1963   "Fictive Kinship in a North Indian Village." *Ethnology*
        2:86–103.
Freed, Ruth S. and Stanley A. Freed
1985   "The Psychomedical Case History of a Low-Caste Woman of
        South India." *Anthropological Papers of the American
        Museum of Natural History,* vol. 60, pt. 2.
Fruzzetti, Lina H.
1980   "Ritual Status of Muslim Women in Rural India." In *Women in
        Contemporary Muslim Societies,* edited by Jane I. Smith, pp.
        186–208. Lewisburg: Bucknell University Press.
Gandhi, Mohandas Karamchand
1957   *An Autobiography. The Story of My Experiments with Truth.*
        Boston: Beacon Press. (First published in 1927).
Goody, Jack
1973   "Bridewealth and Dowry in Africa and Eurasia." In

Bridewealth and Dowry, edited by J. Goody and S. J. Tambish, pp. 1–58. Cambridge: Cambridge University Press.

1976   *Production and Reproduction: a Comparative Study of the Domestic Domain*. Cambridge: Cambridge University Press.

Hershman, Paul

1977   "Virgin and Mother." In *Symbols and Sentiments*, edited by I. Lewis, pp. 269–92. New York: Academic Press.

Hockings, Paul

1987   *Dimensions of Social Life: Essays in Honor of David G. Mandelbaum*. Berlin: Mouton de Gruyter.

Husain, A. F. A.

1958   *Human and Social Impact of Technological Change in Pakistan*. 2 vols. Dacca: Oxford University Press, Pakistan.

Husain, Sheikh Abrar

1976   *Marriage Customs among Muslims in India. A Sociological Study of the Shiah Marriage Customs*. New Delhi: Sterling Publishers.

Jacobson, Doranne

1970   "Hidden Faces: Hindu and Muslim Purdah in a Central Indian Village." Ph.D. diss., Columbia University.

1976a   "The Veil of Virtue: *Purdah* and the Muslim Family in the Bhopal Region of India." In *Family, Kinship, and Marriage Among Muslims in India*, edited by I. Ahmad, pp. 169–216. New Delhi: Manohar.

1976b   "Women and Jewelry in Rural India." In *Family and Social Change in Modern India*, edited by G. R. Gupta, pp. 135–83. New Delhi: Vikas.

1977a   "The Women of North and Central India: Goddesses and Wives." In *Women in India: Two Perspectives*, edited by D. Jacobson and S. S. Wadley, pp. 17–112. New Delhi: Manohar.

1977b   "Indian Women in Processes of Development." *Journal of International Affairs* 30:211–42.

1982   "Purdah and the Hindu Family in Central India." In *Separate Worlds*, edited by H. Papanek and G. Minault, pp. 81–107. Delhi: Chanakya Publications.

Jeffery, Patricia

1979   *Frogs in a Well*. London: Zed Press.

Kakar, Sudhir

1978   *The Inner World. A Psychoanalytic Study of Childhood and Society in India*. Delhi: Oxford University Press.

Karve, Irawati

1962   "On the Road: A Maharashtrian Pilgrimage." *Journal of Asian*

       Studies 22:13–20.

1965   *Kinship Organization in India.* 2d rev. ed. Bombay: Asia
        Publishing House.

1966   "The Indian Women in 1975." *Indian Journal of Public
        Administration Supplement* 1:103–35.

Kolenda, Pauline

1984   "Woman as Tribute, Woman as Flower: Images of 'Woman' in
        Weddings in North and South India." *American Anthropologist*
        11:98–138.

Korson, J. Henry and Michelle Maskiell

1985   "Islamization and Social Policy in Pakistan; The
        Constitutional Crisis and the Status of Women." *Asian Survey*
        25:589–612.

Kressel, Gideon M.

1981   "Sororicide/Filiacide: Homicide for Family Honor." *Current
        Anthropology* 22:141–58.

Krygier, Jocelyn

1982   "Caste and Female Pollution." In *Women in India and Nepal,*
        edited by M. Allen and S. M. Mukherjee, pp. 76–104.
        Australian National University Monograph on South Asia, no.
        8.

Lambert, Ismail A.

1976   "Marriage among the Sunni Surati Vohras of South Gujarat." In
        Family, Kinship, and Marriage among Muslims in India,
        edited by I. Ahmad, pp. 49–82. New Delhi: Manohar.

Leonard, Karen Isaksen

1976   "Women and Social Change in Modern India." *Feminist
        Studies* 3:117–30.

1978   *Social History of an Indian Caste: The Kayasths of Hyderabad.*
        Berkeley: University of California Press.

Lindholm, Charles

1982   *Generosity and Jealousy: The Swat Pukhtun of Northern
        Pakistan.* New York: Columbia University Press.

Lopamudra

1983   "Dowry Death: When Is the End?" *Social Welfare* (New Delhi)
        30:4–5.

Luschinsky, Mildred Stroop

1962   *The Life of Women in a Village of North India: A Study of
        Role and Status.* 2 vols. Ph.D. diss., Cornell University.

Madan, T. N.

1981   "Religious Ideology and Social Structure; the Muslims and
        Hindus of Kashmir." In *Ritual and Religion among Muslims in
        India,* edited by I. Ahmad, pp. 21–64. New Delhi: Manohar.

Makhlouf, Carla
  1979 *Changing Veils, Women and Modernization in North Yemen.*
        Austin: University of Texas Press.
Mandelbaum, David G.
  1938 "Polyandry in Kota Society." *American Anthropologist*
        40:574–83.
  1939a "Agricultural Ceremonies among Three Tribes of Travancore."
        Ethnos 4: 114–28.
  1939b "The Jewish Way of Life in Cochin." *Jewish Social Studies*
        1:423–60.
  1940 *The Plains Cree.* Anthropological Papers of the American
        Museum of Natural History (New York), vol. 37, pt. 2.
  1947 "Hindu-Muslim Conflict in India." *The Middle East Journal*
        1:369–85.
  1952 *Soldier Groups and Negro Soldiers.* Berkeley: University of
        California Press.
  1955a "Psychiatry in Military Society - I." *Human Organization*
        13(3): 5–15.
  1955b "Psychiatry in Military Society - II." *Human Organization*
        13(4): 19–25.
  1965 "Alcohol and Culture." *Current Anthropology* 6:281–92.
  1966 "Transcendental and Pragmatic Aspects of Religion."
        American Anthropologist 68:1174–91.
  1970 *Society in India.* 2 vols. Berkeley and Los Angeles: University
        of California Press.
  1973 "The Study of Life History: Gandhi." *Current Anthropology*
        14:177–206.
  1974 *Human Fertility in India: Social Components and Policy
        Perspectives.* Berkeley: University of California Press.
  1979 *The Plains Cree, an Ethnographic, Historical and Comparative
        Study.* Canadian Plains Studies No. 9. Canadian Plains
        Research Center: University of Regina. (Expanded edition of
        1940.)
  1980 "*The Todas* in Time Perspective." *Reviews in Anthropology*
        7:279–302.
  1982 "Some Shared Ideas." In *Crisis in Anthropology,* edited by E. A.
        Hoebel, R. Currier, and S. Kaiser, pp. 35–50. New
        York: Garland Publishing.
  1984a "Anthropology for the Nuclear Age." *Bulletin of the Atomic
        Scientists* 40:11–15.
  1984b "Anthropology for the Second Stage of the Nuclear Age."
        Economic and Political Weekly. Sept. 8, 1984, pp. 1584–87.
        (Expanded version of 1984a.)

Mandelbaum, David G., Gabriel W. Lasker, and Ethel M. Albert, eds.
   1963a   *The Teaching of Anthropology.* Berkeley: University of
           California Press.
   1963b   *Resources for the Teaching of Anthropology.*
           Berkeley: University of California Press.
Mehta, Rama
   1970   *The Western Educated Hindu Woman.* Bombay: Asia
           Publishing House.
   1982   "Purdah among the Oswals of Mewar." In *Separate Worlds,*
           edited by H. Papanek and G. Minault, pp. 139–63.
Mernissi, Fatima
   1975   *Beyond the Veil, Male-Female Dynamics in a Modernized
           Muslim Society.* New York: John Wiley and Sons.
Metcalf, Barbara Daly, ed.
   1984   "Islamic Reform and Islamic Women: Maulānā Thānawī's
           Jewelry of Paradise." In *Moral Conduct and Authority. The
           Place of Adab in South Asian Islam,* pp. 184–95.
           Berkeley: University of California Press.
Miller, Barbara D.
   1981   *The Endangered Sex, Neglect of Female Children in Rural
           North India.* Ithaca: Cornell University Press.
Minault, Gail
   1973   "Muslim Women in Conflict with Parda: Their Role in the
           Nationalist Movement." Paper presented at the Berkshire
           Conference of Women Historians, New Brunswick, New
           Jersey.
   1982   "Purdah Politics: The Role of Muslim Women in Indian
           Nationalism 1911–1924." In *Separate Worlds,* edited by
           H. Papanek and G. Minault, pp. 245–61. Delhi: Chanakya
           Publications.
Minturn, Leigh and William W. Lambert
   1964   *Mothers of Six Cultures.* New York: John Wiley and Sons.
Minturn, Leigh, and John T. Hitchcock
   1966   *The Rajputs of Khalapur, India.* New York: John Wiley and Sons.
Murphy, Robert
   1964   "Social Distance and the Veil." *American Anthropologist*
           66:1257–74.
Naim, C. M.
   1984   "Prize-Winning Adab: A Study of Five Urdu Books Written in
           Response to the Allahabad Government Gazette Notification."
           In *Moral Conduct and Authority, the Place of Adab in South
           Asian Islam,* edited by B. D. Metcalf, pp. 290–314.
           Berkeley: University of California Press.

Nath, Jharna
   1981   "Beliefs and Customs Observed by Muslim Rural Women
          During Their Life Cycle." In *The Endless Day,* edited by F. S.
          Epstein and R. A. Watts, pp. 13–30. New York: Pergamon
          Press.
Naveed-I-Rahat
   1981   "The Role of Women in Reciprocal Relationships in a Punjab
          Village." In *The Endless Day,* edited by F. S. Epstein and R. A.
          Watts, pp. 47–84. New York: Pergamon Press.
Nazmul Karim, A. K.
   1963   "Changing Patterns of an East Pakistan Family." In *Women in
          the New Asia,* edited by Barbara E. Ward, pp. 292–322.
          Paris: UNESCO.
Nicholas, Ralph
   1965–66   "Economics of Family Types in Two West Bengal Villages."
          In *Seven Articles on Village Conditions,* pp. 33–40. Asian
          Studies Papers. Repr. ser. no. 1. Michigan State University.
Norman, Dorothy
   1965   *Nehru, The First Sixty Years.* 2 vols. New York: John Day Co.
Obeyesekere, Gananath
   1984   *The Cult of the Goddess Pattini.* Chicago and London: The
          University of Chicago Press.
O'Flaherty, Wendy D.
   1980   *Women, Androgynes, and Other Mythical Beasts.*
          Chicago: University of Chicago Press.
Omvedt, Gail
   1980   *We Will Smash This Prison: Indian Women in Struggle.*
          London: Zed Press.
Ortner, Sherry B.
   1972   "Is Female to Male as Nature is to Culture?" *Feminist Studies*
          1:5–31. Reprinted in *Women, Culture, and Society,* edited by
          M. Z. Rosaldo and L. Lamphere, pp. 67–88. Stanford: Stanford
          University Press.
   1978   "The Virgin and the State." *Feminist Studies* 4:19–36.
   1981   "Gender and Sexuality in Hierarchical Societies: the Case of
          Polynesia and Some Comparative Implications." In *Sexual
          Meanings,* edited by S. B. Ortner and H. Whitehead, pp.
          359–409. Cambridge and New York: Cambridge University
          Press.
Ortner, Sherry B., and Harriet Whitehead
   1981   "Introduction: Accounting for Sexual Meaning." In *Sexual*

Meanings. Also edited by Ortner and Whitehead, pp. 1–28.
Cambridge and New York: Cambridge University Press.

Papanek, Hanna
1982 "Purdah: Separate Worlds and Symbolic Shelter." In *Separate Worlds*, edited by H. Papanek and G. Minault, pp. 3–53. Delhi: Chanakya Publications and Columbia, Missouri: South Asia Books. Originally published in *Comparative Studies in Society and History*, vol. 15 (1973), no. 3, pp. 289–325.

Pastner, Carroll McC.
1972 "A Social, Structural and Historical Analysis of Honor, Shame and Purdah." *Anthropological Quarterly* 14:248–59.
1974 "Accommodations to Purdah: The Female Perspective." *Journal of Marriage and the Family* 36:408–14.
1979 "Cousin Marriage among the Zikri Baluch of Coastal Pakistan." *Ethnology* 18:31–47.
1982 "Gradations of Purdah and the Creation of Social Boundaries on a Baluchistan Oasis." In *Separate Worlds*, edited by H. Papanek and G. Minault, pp. 164–89. Delhi: Chanakya Publications and Columbia, Missouri: South Asia Books.

Patai, Raphael
1969 *Golden River to Golden Road*. 3d enlarged ed. Philadelphia: University of Pennsylvania Press.

Pettigrew, Joyce
1975 *Robber Noblemen: A Study of the Political System of the Sikh Jats*. London: Routledge and Kegan Paul.

Pyarelal (Nair)
1965 *Mahatma Gandhi*, vol. 1. *The Early Phase*. Ahmedabad: Nanjivam Publishing House.

Radcliffe-Brown, A. R.
1952 *Structure and Function in Primitive Society*. London: Cohen and West.

Rahman, Fazlur
1982 "The Status of Women in Islam: A Modernist Interpretation." In *Separate Worlds*, edited by H. Papanek and G. Minault, pp. 285–310. Delhi: Chanakya Publications.

Rajaram, Indira
1983 "Economics of Bride-Price and Dowry." *Economic and Political Weekly* (Bombay) 18:275–79.

Randeria, Shalini, and Leela Visaria
1984 "Sociology of Bride-Price and Dowry." *Economic and Political Weekly* 19:648–52.

Rivers, W. H. R.
  1906   *The Todas.* New York: Macmillan and Co.
Rizvi, S. M. Akram
  1976   "Kinship and Industry among the Muslim Karkhanedars in
          Delhi." In *Family, Kinship, and Marriages among Muslims in
          India,* edited by Imtiaz Ahmad, pp. 27–48. New
          Delhi: Manohar.
Rosaldo, Michelle Z.
  1974   "Women, Culture, and Society, A Theoretical Overview." In
          Women, Culture, and Society, edited by M. Z. Rosaldo and
          L. Lamphere. Stanford: Stanford University Press.
Roy, Shibani
  1979   *Status of Muslim Women in North India.* Delhi: B. R.
          Publishing Corp.
Rubin, Gayle
  1975   "The Traffic in Women: Notes Toward a Political Economy of
          Sex." In *Toward an Anthropology of Women,* edited by
          R. Reiter, pp. 157–210. New York: Monthly Review Press.
Saiyal, A. R.
  1976   "Purdah, Family Structure and the Status of Woman: A Note
          on a Deviant Case." In *Family, Kinship and Marriage among
          Muslims in India,* edited by I. Ahmad, pp. 239–264. New
          Delhi: Manohar.
Sakala, Carol
  1980   *Women of South Asia: A Guide to Resources.* Millwood, New
          York: Krause International.
Sanday, Peggy R.
  1973   "Toward a Theory of the Status of Women." *American
          Anthropologist* 75:1682–1700.
Sapir, Edward
  1949   *Selected Writings of Edward Sapir.* Edited by David G.
          Mandelbaum. Berkeley: University of California Press.
Seymour, Susan
  1975   "Child Rearing in India: A Case Study in Change and
          Modernization." In *Socialization and Communication in
          Primary Groups,* edited by T. R. Williams, pp. 40–58.
          Chicago: Aldine.
Sharma, Ursula
  1978   "Women and Their Affines: The Veil as a Symbol of
          Separation." *Man in India,* 13:218–33.

1980   *Women, Work, and Property in North-West India.* London and
        New York: Tavistock Publications.

Sopher, David E.

1980   "The Geographical Patterning of Culture in India." In *An
        Exploration of India, Geographical Perspective on Society and
        Culture*, also edited by Sopher, pp. 289–326. Ithaca: Cornell
        University Press.

"S.V."

1984   "Dowry Amendment Bill." *Economic and Political Weekly*
        19:1609–10.

Tambiah, S. J.

1973   "Dowry and Bridewealth and the Property Rights of Women in
        South Asia." In *Bridewealth and Dowry*, edited by J. Goody
        and S. J. Tambiah, pp. 59–169. Cambridge and New
        York: Cambridge University Press.

Towards Equality

1974   *Report on the Committee on the Status of Women in India.*
        New Delhi: Department of Social Welfare, Government of
        India.

Ullah, Inayat

1958   "Caste, Patti and Faction in the Life of a Punjabi Village."
        Sociologus: 8:170–86.

Vatuk, Sylvia

1972   *Kinship and Urbanization, White Collar Migrants in North
        India.* Berkeley and Los Angeles: University of California
        Press.

1975   "The Aging Woman in India: Self-Perceptions and Changing
        Roles." In *Women in Contemporary India*, edited by A. de
        Souza, pp. 142–163. Delhi: Manohar.

1982   "Purdah Revisited: A Comparison of Hindu and Muslim
        Interpretations of the Cultural Meanings of Purdah in South
        Asia." In *Separate Worlds*, edited by Hanna Papanek and Gail
        Minault, pp. 54–78. Delhi: Chanakya Publications.

Vreede-de Stuers, Cora

1968   *Parda: A Study of Muslim Women's Life in Northern India.*
        Assen: Van Gorcum and Co.

Wadley, Susan S.

1977   "Women and the Hindu Tradition." In *Women in India: Two
        Perspectives*, edited by D. Jacobson and S. Wadley, pp. 113–140.
        New Delhi: Manohar.

Wadley, Susan S.
1980   "The Powers of Tamil Women." Foreign and Comparative
Studies/South Asian Series, no. 6. Maxwell School, Syracuse
University, Syracuse, N. Y.

Wasi, Muriel
1971   "Who is the Educated Woman of India Today?" In *The
Educated Woman in Indian Society Today*, edited by M. Wasi,
pp. 7–17. Bombay-New Delhi: Tata McGraw-Hill.

Weiss, Anita
1985   "Women's Position: Socio-Cultural Effects of Islamization."
Asian Survey 25:863–80.

Whiting, Beatrice B.
1965   "Sex Identity, Conflict and Physical Violence." In *The
Ethnography of Law*, edited by L. Nader, pp. 123–40. American
Anthropologist vol. 67, pt. 2.

Whiting, Beatrice B., and J. W. M. Whiting
1975   *Children of Six Cultures: A Psycho-Cultural Analysis.*
Cambridge: Harvard University Press.

Wikan, Unni
1980   *Life Among the Poor in Cairo.* New York: Tavistock
Publications.

Wiser, William H., and Charlotte W. Wiser
1963   *Behind Mud Walls.* Berkeley and Los Angeles: University of
California Press.

Yalman, Nur O.
1963   "On the Purity of Women in the Castes of Ceylon and
Malabar." *Journal of the Royal Anthropological Institute*
93:25–58.

Yunus, Reshma
1983   Unpublished Field notes on interviews with Muslim women in
the San Francisco Bay Area.

Zaidi, S. M. Hafeez
1970   *The Village Culture in Transition, A Study of East Pakistan
Rural Society.* Honolulu: East-West Center Press.

INDEX

Uttar Pradesh, 27

Vatuk, Sylvia, 4, 37, 39, 47
Veil: "indoor veil," 103; manipulation of, 51–52; symbolism of, 103–4
Vengeance, 94
Village society, 15–16, 36–37, 63–64, 120
Virginity, 73–74, 101
Visaria, Leela, 66
Visiting, 6–7, 49, 53
Vote, 7
Vreede-de Stuers, Cora, 6, 44

Wadley, Susan S., 31, 32
Wages, 34, 64
Wasi, Muriel, 117
We Will Smash This Prison (Omvedt), 122
Weddings, 28–31, 112. *See also* Marriage; Muslims/Hindus compared
Weiss, Anita, 123
Wheat, 32, 64, 129
White-collar neighborhoods, 37–

38, 39
Whitehead, Harriet, 99, 101, 118
Whiting, Beatrice, 54, 55
Whiting, John, 54
Wiser, Charlotte, 74
Withdrawal of sexual favors, 52n
Wives, 5, 73–74, 122; junior wives, 13–14, 30, 31
Women: attitudes of toward purdah, 47–48, 50, 51, 116–17; attitudes toward, 100–101; characterization of, 99–100; dual nature of, 73–75; improvements for, 88–91, 115–17; senior women, 19, 25, 47; separate world of, 4–5, 104, 106–7; social networks of, 40–41
Women's movement, 116, 117
Women's organizations, 124

Yunus, Reshma, 80, 82

Zaidi, S. M. Hafeez, 82
Zenana (women's quarters), 80
Zikri Baluch, 91

About the Author

DAVID G. MANDELBAUM
was the first American anthropologist to do fieldwork in India. He was
Professor of Anthropology at the University of California, Berkeley, for
more than forty years, until his retirement in 1978. He was a professor
emeritus until his death in 1987. During his career, he was author of
numerous books including the two-volume *Society in India* (1970),
The Plains Cree (1940, 1979), and *Human Fertility in India* (1974).